THE
Women's Institute
BOOK OF
Preserves
&
Pickles

THE WOMEN'S INSTITUTES

The WI was formed in 1915 to revitalize rural communities and encourage women to become more involved in producing food during the First World War. Since then the organization's aims have broadened and the WI is now the largest voluntary women's organization in the UK. The WI will celebrate its centenary in 2015 and currently has 212,000 members in around 6,600 WIs. The WI plays a unique role in providing women with educational opportunities and the chance to build new skills, to take part in a wide variety of activities and to campaign on issues that matter to them and their communities.

For further information, please contact:

The National Federation of Women's Institutes
104 New Kings Road
London
SW6 4LY

Tel: 020 7371 9300
Fax: 020 7371 0912
Email: hq@nfwi.org.uk

www.theWI.org.uk

THE
Women's Institute
BOOK OF
Preserves
&
Pickles

ℬℬ Bounty
Books

The recipes collected in this book represent many decades of WI cooking so some of the methods and ingredients may be unfamiliar. Where possible, for hard to find ingredients, we have suggested a more modern alternative.

First published in Great Britain in 1978 by Macdonald Educational Limited as *Preserves and Preserving*

This edition published in 2015 by Bounty Books, a division of Octopus Publishing Group Ltd Endeavour House, 189 Shaftesbury Avenue, London WC2H 8JY www.octopusbooks.co.uk

An Hachette UK Company www.hachette.co.uk

ISBN: 978-0-753727-37-9

A CIP catalogue record for this book is available from the British Library

Printed and bound in China

Picture credits
Every effort has been made to trace the copyright holders, and we apologise in advance for any unintentional omissions. We would be pleased to insert the appropriate acknowledgement in any subsequent edition of this publication.

All images by Shutterstock: 3 (and repeats) geraria; 8 Pavel K; 9 schab; 11 Ohn Mar; 17 Ksusha Dusmikeeva; 23 Ohn Mar; 27 alekup; 31 Gergana Todorchovska 41 Gergana Todorchovska; 42 Gergana Todorchovska; 45 Ksusha Dusmikeeva; 46 andrey oleynik; 54 geraria; 57 andrey oleynik; 62 Pavel K; 71 Ksusha Dusmikeeva; 78 Gergana Todorchovska; 79 Ohn Mar; 95 Gergana Todorchovska; 113 Gergana Todorchovska; 115 geraria; 125 iralu; 126 Ohn Mar; 156 Liliya Shlapak; 187 Liliya Shlapak

Contents

Introduction

THE SKILLS of preservation have been known and used in the UK and throughout the world for centuries, and the range of fruit, vegetables, herbs, meat and fish preserved in one form or another has widened enormously since Roman times.

Our ancestors had a difficult job, for their methods of preservation were the natural ones: sun, wind, smoke and salt. Meat and fish were hung near a fire or inside a chimney well away from flies and insects. In this way, the food was dried and often smoked as well. Hours of soaking were necessary when the meat or fish was required for use but, at least, preserving helped to ensure a regular supply of food throughout the year.

In the hotter climates of the world, fruit and vegetables were spread out to dry in the sun and, even today, this method of preservation is used.

Salt, both as a method of preservation and as part of man's diet, has through many ages been regarded as a valuable world-wide commodity in trading and bartering. From medieval times onwards, we find it listed in household accounts.

The Romans are generally thought to have been responsible for the introduction of orchards (the growing of fruit trees and bushes together near the house) as well as herb and vegetable gardens, but it is from the Middle Ages onwards that we read of the housewife's 'still-room' and its rows of preserves. The containers were covered with cloths dipped in mutton fat or 'swine's grease'. At this period, and until well into the eighteenth century, the only sweetening agent was honey but, when sugar became generally available, a much wider variety of preserves was developed.

Although cooking today, both in quantity and style, is very different from what it once was, many of the reasons why the housewife 'preserved' in past centuries still hold good.

The object of preservation is to take food at its maximum freshness and nutritive value and keep it at this stage. All food consists of organic materials, which go through a natural cycle of development and decay, and which eventually cause the food to be unfit for consumption.

We still use drying and smoking as methods of preservation but today sugar, salt, vinegar and alcohol, together with the application of heat or cold, are the main preserving agents. We now know *why* food goes bad, thanks to the enormous advances in food technology over the last 100–150 years. As a result, the housewife can now preserve and store an ever-widening range of fruit, vegetables and herbs and, in this way, can provide a wider variety of flavours and tasty additions to meals during the months when the fresh items are not available. Many of these fruits and vegetables are also an important source of Vitamin C.

Farmers and gardeners do their best to prolong the growing season to provide a succession of crops but, even so, we have times of gluts and shortages. At glut periods, the housewife can preserve the surplus whether from her own or a friend's garden. It can also be economical to take advantage of any glut offers in the shops and buy in your fruit and vegetables.

Preservation is a creative art and an enormous amount of pleasure and satisfaction is gained in producing preserves well below shop prices, with a flavour and colour no commercial product can match. As your experience grows, you will be able to experiment with combinations of fruit, vegetables, herbs and spices to produce your own individual recipes.

Jams, Jellies, Marmalades & Curds

Jams

JAM is a preserve produced by boiling fruit with sugar. (The name is supposed to have come from the 'jamming' or bruising together of the fruit and sugar.) When honey was the only source of sweetening, a conserve was the nearest to our present-day jam. This consisted of pieces of fruit in a thick syrup.

Jam should be well set but not too stiff and, most important, it should have a distinct fruity flavour, true to the fruit used.

Jam-making is one of the most usual methods of preserving fruit, and is still greatly practised, in spite of the considerably increased popularity of freezing in recent times. However, shelves of home-made jams can still be a great source of satisfaction to the housewife.

Equipment

Preserving pan A good quality, heavy, aluminium or stainless steel pan is best, because the heavy base helps to prevent burning. The pan should be deep enough to prevent fruit boiling over and wide enough to allow for evaporation. A heavy-based saucepan, 4.2–4.8-litre (7–8-pint) size, can be used for making *small* quantities of jam but a good preserving pan is an investment that will last a lifetime. A pressure cooker, used without the lid, can also be used for making small quantities of jam. Copper jam pans are no longer recommended for use because the copper destroys the Vitamin C present in the fruit.

Scales Preferably with both metric and imperial measurements.

Bowls or basins Earthenware, enamel, plastic, glass or Pyrex.

Sieves Nylon or stainless steel.

Measuring jug Heatproof glass, stainless steel or enamel.

Spoons Long-handled wooden for stirring and perforated stainless steel for removing scum and stones.

Knives and peelers With stainless steel blades, to prevent discoloration of fruit.

Jam jars and covers With the many variations in jar sizes and tops, it is advisable to keep a selection of packets of transparent cellulose covers with wax-coated discs, plastic-coated twist tops, and packets of plastic skin (which can be cut to size). Fine string is preferable for tying down transparent cellulose and plastic skin tops. Rubber bands tend to perish during storage and are therefore not very satisfactory.

Sugar thermometer Useful, but not essential.

Wide-necked funnel A help when filling jam jars but not essential.

Grater Double-sided, fine and coarse; stainless steel is preferable.

Pectin

Wash and pick over fruit before use and discard any that is over-ripe or decayed. Always use fruit that is firm, fresh and just ripe or slightly under-ripe; over-ripe fruit will have lost much of its pectin content.

Pectin is a natural substance contained in fruit which helps the jam to 'set'. It is contained in greatly varying quantity in different fruits.

Good pectin content:
black and red currants
cooking apples
damsons
gooseberries
plums (some varieties)
quince
strawberries

Medium pectin content:
apricots, fresh
blackberries, early
greengages
loganberries
raspberries

Poor pectin content:
blackberries, late
cherries
elderberries
medlars
pears
rhubarb

The pectin content of fruit is reduced during freezing, so if you are using frozen fruit for jams, jellies and curds, increase the quantity specified in the recipe by 10 per cent to offset the loss. When using frozen citrus fruits, increase the quantity by one-eighth.

Recipes using fruit of low pectin content often have acid added in the form of *pectin stock*. This can be homemade or prepared commercially, and basically comprises the juice of pectin-rich fruits. Citric acid is often added to fruits low in acid (which are often those that are low in pectin too) and it also helps to give a good 'set'.

Pectin Test

A test for pectin content can be made after the first cooking (i.e. before the sugar is added) by taking a 1 x 5 ml spoon (1 teaspoon) of juice from the pan, placing it in a glass or small jar and cooling. Add 1 x 15 ml spoon (1 tablespoon) of methylated spirit and shake gently together. If plenty of pectin is present, a large, clear, jelly-like clot will form. If there is a medium amount of pectin, several small clots will form. If there is very little pectin, no real clots form at all. In this case, additional pectin will have to be added in the form of apple, redcurrant or gooseberry juice.

Sugar

It is not essential to use preserving sugar; just ordinary granulated, whether cane or beet, is quite adequate. Preserving or lump sugar creates less scum, but the amount of scum can be lessened considerably by adding a nut of butter or a few drops of glycerine to the jam during the cooking process. Do not use brown sugar, unless specified in a recipe, because it alters, and can even mask, the flavour of the fruit.

The amount of sugar needed to set the jam depends on the amount of pectin present in the fruit, so always use the amount specified in the recipe. Too little sugar will result in a poor set and runny jam. More sugar and further cooking should remedy this. Too much sugar will produce a dark and sticky jam and the true flavour of the fruit will be lost.

Put sugar in the oven to warm before adding it to jam. This reduces the cooking time considerably, giving better colour and flavour. It is particularly helpful for raspberry and strawberry jams.

Always make certain sugar is fully dissolved before bringing the jam to the boil, otherwise the texture of the jam will be granular and the set poor. The less boiling of the jam after the addition of the sugar, the better the colour and flavour will be. Prolonged boiling darkens the colour, affects the flavour, and the 'jelling' properties begin to disappear.

General Points

•   As a general rule, soft juicy fruits such as strawberries, raspberries, blackberries and loganberries do not need any water added to them throughout the cooking process.

•   When trying a recipe for the first time, never make a large quantity. Wait and see whether the family likes it.

•   Jam benefits from being made in small quantities (up to 5 kg or 10 lb) as the less time spent in cooking, the better the colour and flavour.

•   When making jams, never cover the pan unless the recipe instructs you to do so, since evaporation of the water content is an important part of the cooking process.

Setting Point for Jam

The two easiest methods of testing for setting are the 'flake' test and the 'cold saucer' test. Always remove the pan from the heat when testing for set.

The 'flake' test Dip a clean wooden spoon into the jam. Hold the spoon over the pan and twist it to cool the jam, then allow the cooling jam to drop from the edge of the spoon. If drops of jam run together and form 'flakes' which hang on the edge of the spoon and then cut away cleanly, setting point has been reached.

The 'cold saucer' test Put 1 x 5 ml spoon (1 teaspoon) of jam on a saucer, allow to cool for 1 minute, then push the surface gently with your finger tip. If the surface wrinkles, setting point has been reached. If you chill the saucer in the refrigerator before use, this will speed up cooling of the jam.

If you are using a sugar thermometer to test for set, stir the jam and then remove it from the heat. Dip the thermometer in hot water, then submerge the bulb fully in the jam. If the thermometer registers 105°C, 220°F, the jam is then ready.

When making jam, be sure you have enough clean, warm and dry jars and appropriate tops ready.

Sterilizing Jars

It is important that jars and lids are sterilized before filling with preserves or pickles. You should aim to finish sterilizing at the same time as the preserve is ready to be potted – the hot preserve should be potted into clean, warm, dry jars (unless the recipe specifies otherwise).

There are three ways to sterilize:

1. Lay the jars and lids in a large saucepan, cover with cold water and put on the saucepan lid. Bring to the boil over a high heat and boil for 20 minutes.
2. Put the jars and lids through the hottest dishwasher cycle, without detergent.

3. Set the oven to the lowest possible temperature. Place the jars upright on a wooden board or baking tray on the lowest shelf of the oven, close the oven door and heat the jars for 30 minutes.

When ready to pot the preserve, protecting your hands from the heat, remove the jars and lids from the boiling water, dishwasher or oven and stand upright. Any water in the jars will evaporate quite quickly.

Storage

All jams are best stored in a dry, cool and dark place, as excess of heat, light and damp can affect them. Heat makes the contents shrink, light can fade the colour and sparkle and damp may cause moulds to grow on the surface of the jam.

Storage of jams in centrally heated homes is a problem; it is advisable to use jars with twist-tops, since these form an airtight seal and therefore prevent moisture from evaporating.

It is a good idea to check over your stock of jams from time to time, particularly if storage conditions are not ideal.

Entering Preserves for Competition or Show

Read the schedule for the show or competition carefully to make sure that you fully understand the rules.

Use jars free from blemishes or marks and without proprietary brand labels, etc. Use a suitable container for the type of preserve: i.e., do not use pickle jars, fish paste jars, etc. for jams. Label jars with the type of preserve and date and keep the label straight and free from wrinkles. Jars should be filled right to the brim.

Use properly fitting wax discs under transparent cellulose covers. The correct application of these discs is important. They must be placed in position immediately a jar is filled, and must cover the surface of the jam completely. This helps in keeping the preserve and shows that the competitor understands the principles of preservation.

Transparent cellulose covers can be put on either at once or when the jam is cold and set. Trim the transparent cellulose or plastic skin covers carefully after the jam has cooled and set.

Plastic-coated twist tops do not require a waxed disc on top of the preserve but should be placed on a jar immediately it is filled, so as to form an airtight seal. Do not use lined screw tops with a wax disc, except as a 'dust cover'.

Clean and polish the outside of the jars or bottles. A cloth, moistened with a few drops of methylated spirit, is excellent for giving a sparkling finish to all glass containers. Handle the container carefully after polishing, to prevent finger marking.

Apricot Jam using Fresh Fruit

The addition of a few kernels is optional here but it does give a distinctive flavour to the jam. Never use more than two or three in a recipe.

MAKES APPROX. 4.5 KG (10 LB)
3 kg (6 lb) apricots
600 ml (1 pint) water
3 kg (6 lb) sugar

Wash the fruit and drain well, then halve and remove the stones. Place the fruit and water in a pan. Crack a few of the stones, remove the kernels and add to the pan.

Simmer until the apricots are tender and the contents of the pan are reduced by about one-third. Test for pectin, then remove from the heat. Add the sugar and stir until dissolved. Return to the heat and bring to boiling point. Boil hard until setting point is reached. Pot into warm jars and cover.

Apricot Jam using Dried Fruit

The almonds are optional but give an attractive flavour and
appearance to this jam.

MAKES APPROX. 4.5 KG (10 LB)
1 kg (2 lb) dried apricots
3.5 litres (6 pints) water
juice of 2 lemons
or 2 x 5 ml spoons (2 teaspoons) citric acid
75 g (3 oz) almonds
3 kg (6 lb) sugar

Wash the apricots and soak in water to cover for 24–36 hours. Drain and place in a pan with the measured water and the lemon juice or citric acid. Simmer for 30 minutes. Meanwhile, blanch the almonds, then shred or halve them.

Remove the jam from the heat and add the sugar and almonds. Stir until the sugar has dissolved, then return to the heat and bring to boiling point. Boil hard until setting point is reached. Pot into warm jars and cover.

Apricot Jam for Competition

If entering apricot jam for competition or show, remember to state on the label whether dried or fresh fruit was used, as the colour does vary.

Blackcurrant Jam

MAKES APPROX. 4.5 KG (10 LB)
2 kg (4 lb) blackcurrants
1.5 litres (3 pints) water
3 kg (6 lb) sugar

Remove the stalks from the blackcurrants (stranding the stems through the prongs of a fork will speed this process), then wash and drain. Place in a pan with the water. Simmer gently until the fruit is tender, and the contents of the pan are reduced by about one-third. Stir frequently as the pulp thickens to prevent sticking.

Test for pectin. Remove from the heat, add the sugar and stir until dissolved. Return to the heat and bring to boiling point. Boil hard until setting point is reached. Pot into warm jars and cover.

Cooking Blackcurrants for Jam

Blackcurrants and similar tough-skinned fruit must be cooked well before the sugar is added, otherwise they will look like boot buttons in the jam. Once sugar has been added to fruit, it toughens the tissue and no amount of boiling will soften the fruit.

Blackberry & Apple Jam

Either cultivated or wild blackberries can be used in this recipe,
but wild ones give a better flavour.

MAKES APPROX. 4.5 KG (10 LB)
2 kg (4 lb) blackberries
300 ml (½ pint) water
1 kg (2 lb) cooking apples
3 kg (6 lb) sugar

Wash and drain the blackberries, then put in a pan with half the water.
Simmer until soft. Peel, core and chop the apples and simmer in the
remainder of the water until soft. Mix the two fruits together and test
for pectin. Remove the pan from the heat and add the sugar. Stir until
dissolved. Return to the heat and bring the jam to the boil. Boil hard
until setting point is reached. Pot into warm jars and cover.

For a seedless jam, sieve the cooked blackberries before mixing with the
softened apples, and reduce the sugar to 2.25 kg (4½ lb)

Raspberry Jam

MAKES APPROX. 4.5 KG (10 LB)
3 kg (6 lb) raspberries
3 kg (6 lb) sugar

Wash the fruit if necessary, drain well and place in a pan. Simmer gently
until some juice has been extracted, then test for pectin. Remove from
the heat and add the sugar. Stir until dissolved. Return to the heat and
bring to the boil. Boil hard until setting point is reached. Pot into warm
jars and cover.

Strawberry Jam

Choose small- to medium-size fruit for making this jam.

MAKES APPROX. 4.5 KG (10 LB)
3 kg (6 lb) strawberries
juice of 2 lemons
3 kg (6 lb) sugar

Hull the strawberries, rinse if necessary, drain well and place in a pan with the lemon juice. Simmer gently until reduced by about one-third, stirring occasionally. Remove from the heat and add the sugar. Stir until dissolved. Return to the heat and bring to the boil. Boil hard until setting point is reached. Pot into warm jars and cover.

Good-looking Strawberry Jam

Always allow strawberry jam to cool for 10 minutes and then stir before potting. This distributes the fruit evenly in the jar. If using jars with twist tops, however, the jam must be potted and sealed when hot.

Grape Jam

This jam has a jelly-like consistency in which the fruit floats.
Be sure to use the small, green, seedless grapes stipulated in the
ingredients. These have a higher acid content than other grapes,
and so help to give a better set.

MAKES APPROX. 1.5 KG (3 LB)
2 kg (4 lb) small, green, seedless grapes
1 kg (2 lb) sugar
juice of 2 lemons

Stalk the grapes and rinse well. Drain and place in a pan with the sugar
and lemon juice. Heat slowly, stirring until the sugar has dissolved, then
bring to the boil and boil hard until setting point is reached. Allow to
cool for 5–8 minutes, then stir to distribute the fruit evenly. Pot into
warm jars and cover. The jelly will be a clear pinky-red colour.

Marrow & Ginger Jam

The amount of ginger used in this recipe ensures a good ginger flavour!
Just use less if you would rather the taste were less pronounced.

MAKES APPROX. 4.5 KG (10 LB)
3 kg (6 lb) marrow
4 lemons
250 g (8 oz) crystallized ginger
50 g (2 oz) dried root ginger
3 kg (6 lb) sugar

Peel the marrow and discard the seeds. Cut into cubes and boil or steam
until tender. Drain well and mash. Grate the lemon rind and squeeze
the juice. Finely chop the crystallized ginger. Bruise the root ginger with
a hammer and wrap in a piece of muslin or fine cotton. Put the lemon

rind and juice and the crystallized and root ginger in a pan with the mashed marrow. Bring to simmering point. Add the sugar and stir until dissolved. Bring to the boil and boil for 20 minutes, stirring occasionally as the pulp thickens and setting point is reached (test for this by the temperature). Remove the muslin bag. Pot into warm jars and cover.

Gooseberry Jam

MAKES APPROX. 4.5 KG (10 LB)
2.25 kg (4½ lb) gooseberries
900 ml (1½ pints) water
3 kg (6 lb) sugar

Top and tail the gooseberries, then wash and drain thoroughly. Put in a pan with the water and simmer gently until the skins burst and the fruit has pulped. Test for pectin. Remove from the heat, add the sugar and stir until dissolved. Return to the heat and bring to the boil. Boil hard until setting point is reached. Pot into warm jars and cover.

Green-coloured Gooseberry Jam

For a green jam for exhibition or competition, use young, unripe gooseberries. Make sure that the fruit is cooked before adding warmed sugar.

Apple & Ginger Jam

MAKES APPROX. 4.5 KG (10 LB)
3 kg (6 lb) apples
1 litre (2 pints) water
4 lemons
50 g (2 oz) ground ginger
3 kg (6 lb) sugar
250–500 g (8 oz–1 lb) crystalized ginger (according to taste)

Peel, core and slice the apples. Tie the peel and cores in muslin and place in a pan with the apple slices and water. Grate the rind from the lemons and squeeze the juice. Add this to the pan with the ground ginger. Bring to the boil, stirring occasionally, then cook gently until the apples are soft. Remove from the heat, discard the muslin bag and add the sugar and chopped crystallized ginger. Stir until dissolved. Return to the heat and bring to the boil. Boil until setting point is reached, stirring occasionally. Pot into warm jars and cover.

Ambrosia Jam

The yield from this recipe will vary according to the amount of sugar added (see method). To assess how much you will make assume it will be 1⅔ the amount of sugar added.

1 kg (2 lb) dried apricots
1 orange
1 lemon
1 x 700–800 g (24–28 oz) can crushed pineapple
sugar

Cover the apricots with cold water and leave to soak for 12–24 hours. Drain well, then chop. Grate the orange and lemon rinds and squeeze the juices. Weigh the soaked apricots, orange and lemon rinds and juice, and the drained pineapple and put in a pan with an equal weight of sugar. Heat slowly until the sugar has dissolved, stirring occasionally. Bring to the boil and boil hard for 20–25 minutes or until setting point is reached. Pot into warm jars and cover.

Marrow & Pineapple Jam

This jam does not normally 'set' but makes a delicious filling for tartlets.

marrow
sugar
lemons
canned pineapple chunks or crushed pineapple

Peel, seed and cut the marrow into bite-size chunks. Allowing 350 g (12 oz) sugar to each 500 g (1 lb) marrow, layer together in a bowl. Cover and leave overnight.

Next day add the juice of 1 lemon to every 2 kg (4 lb) marrow and the drained pineapple chunks (cut into four) or crushed pineapple. Allow approximately 500 g (1 lb) pineapple to every 2 kg (4 lb) marrow. Tip the mixture into a saucepan and bring to the boil, stirring until the sugar has dissolved. Boil hard until the chunks of marrow are almost transparent and the syrup thick. Pot into warm jars and cover.

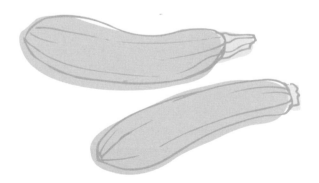

Rhubarb & Ginger Jam

Remove leaves and stalks of the rhubarb before weighing it.

MAKES APPROX. 2.5 KG (5 LB)
1.5 kg (3 lb) rhubarb
1.5 kg (3 lb) sugar
juice of 3 lemons
25 g (1 oz) dried root ginger

Wash the rhubarb and cut into chunks. Layer with the sugar in a large bowl. Pour the lemon juice on top and leave to stand overnight. The next day, tip the contents of the bowl into a pan. Bruise the ginger with a hammer and tie in muslin. Add to the pan. Bring to the boil and boil hard until setting point is reached. Remove the ginger. Pot into warm jars and cover.

All-the-year-round or Medicinal Jam

This jam, which is similar to the prune or plum conserve eaten in Europe, is delicious with wholemeal or brown bread.

MAKES APPROX. 1.5 KG (3 LB)
500 g (1 lb) prunes
500 g (1 lb) seedless raisins
125 g (4 oz) whole almonds
600 ml (1 pint) water
500 g (1 lb) demerara sugar

Wash and stone the prunes. Chop them and the raisins, adding a few kernels from the prune stones if liked. Blanch the almonds, then peel and chop them. Add to the fruit and pour over the water. Leave to soak overnight. Next day, transfer to a pan and add the sugar. Heat gently, stirring until the sugar has dissolved, then boil gently for 25–30 minutes or until setting point is reached. Pot into warm jars and cover.

Black Cherry Conserve

This makes a delicious filling for a sweet pastry flan or tartlets, with a topping of whipped cream. It does not set stiffly like an ordinary jam.

MAKES APPROX. 1.25 KG (2½ LB)
1 kg (2 lb) black or dark cherries
1 kg (2 lb) sugar
75 ml (3 fl oz) redcurrant juice

Wash and stone the cherries. Dissolve the sugar in the redcurrant juice in a pan. Bring to the boil, then drop in the fruit. Cook for 10 minutes, stirring constantly. Skim if necessary with a perforated spoon. Remove the cherries and boil the juice hard for a further 12–15 minutes or until it begins to thicken. Return the cherries to the pan and boil again for a further 12 minutes or until setting point is reached. Allow the conserve to cool (unless using jars with twist tops, in which case pot while still hot) and stir well before potting into warm jars and covering.

Exhibiting Black Cherry Conserve

Do not enter black cherry conserve in a jam class at an exhibition or competition – a conserve does not have the same consistency as a jam.

Apricot Conserve

This makes a delicious filling for brandy snaps or a Swiss roll.

MAKES APPROX. 1.5–2 KG (3–4 LB)
500 g (1 lb) apricots
1.5 litres (3 pints) water
2 oranges
1.5 kg (3 lb) sugar
juice of 2 lemons
50 g (2 oz) walnuts or seedless raisins, whichever is preferred

Cover the apricots with the water. Peel and slice the oranges (putting the pips into a muslin or fine cotton bag) and add to the apricots. Leave to soak for 48 hours. Remove the bag of pips.

Transfer to a pan and simmer gently until soft. Remove from the heat, add the sugar and stir until dissolved, then add the lemon juice. Chop the walnuts or raisins and add to the pan. Return to the heat, bring to the boil and boil hard until setting point is reached (but remember it will be runnier than jam). Pot into warm jars and cover.

Gooseberry & Strawberry Jam

MAKES APPROX. 4.5 KG (10 LB)
1. 5 kg (3 lb) gooseberries
200 ml (7 fl oz) water
1. 5 kg (3 lb) strawberries
3 kg (6 lb) sugar

Wash, top and tail the gooseberries and simmer in the water until they have broken up and are tender. Hull the strawberries and wash if necessary, draining well. Add these to the pan and simmer for a further 2–3 minutes.

Remove from the heat, add the sugar and stir until dissolved. Return to the heat, bring to the boil and continue boiling until setting point is reached, stirring occasionally. Pot into warm jars and cover.

Rhubarb & Peel Jam

MAKES APPROX. 4 KG (8 LB)
3 kg (6 lb) rhubarb
500 g (1 lb) mixed candied peel
1 lemon
3 kg (6 lb) sugar

Trim the leaves and stalk ends of the rhubarb and wipe with a damp cloth. Cut into chunks and place in a pan with the candied peel. Grate the rind from the lemon and squeeze the juice. Add the rind and juice to the pan. Heat gently, stirring occasionally.

Add the sugar and stir to dissolve. Bring to the boil and cook until the jam has thickened. (This jam does not set stiffly, but has a good, spreadable consistency.) Pot into warm jars and cover.

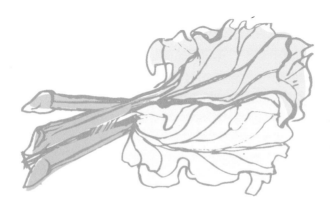

Potted Raspberries

This is not a true jam as the sugar and fruit are not boiled together, so do not enter this in a jam class for show or competition. You must also use plastic twist-top lids, as the jam will not keep under a wax disc and cellophane.

The preserve does not set like ordinary jam: the fruit tends to rise and the juice sets in a jelly-like consistency below. When wanted for use, just open the jar and stir. Once open, keep in the refrigerator. The true raspberry flavour and colour keep for up to 4 months.

This recipe makes 4 kg (8 lb) of preserve – this yield being so high because no water is boiled off in the making process.

2 kg (4 lb) firm dry raspberries
2 kg (4 lb) caster sugar

Do not wash the raspberries unless it is essential to do so. Place the fruit in one heatproof bowl and the sugar in another. Heat both in a warm oven for 20 minutes, or until the juice has just started to run from the berries. Tip the warmed sugar into the berries and mix well until it dissolves, using a wooden spoon. Pot into warm jars and cover.

Quince Jam

MAKES APPROX. 3 KG (6 LB)
2 kg (4 lb) quinces
2 litres (4 pints) water
juice of 2 lemons
3 kg (6 lb) sugar

Peel the quinces and cut up, discarding the woody cores. Place in a pan with the water and lemon juice and bring to the boil. Simmer gently until the fruit is tender and the liquid is reduced by about one-third.

Add the sugar; stir until it has dissolved, then boil hard until setting point is reached. Pot into warm jars and cover.

Plum Jam

MAKES APPROX. 4.5 KG (10 LB)
3 kg (6 lb) plums
600 ml (1 pint) water
3 kg (6 lb) sugar

Wash the plums. Halve them and remove the stones. Place in a pan with the water and add a few kernels if you want to give the jam a distinctive flavour. Simmer until the fruit is tender, then test for pectin. Remove from the heat, add the sugar and stir until dissolved. Return to the heat and bring to the boil. Boil hard until setting point is reached. Pot into warm jars and cover.

Tutti-Frutti Jam

MAKES APPROX. 3 KG (6 LB)
500 g (1 lb) blackcurrants
500 g (1 lb) redcurrants
500 g (1 lb) strawberries
500 g (1 lb) raspberries
water
2 kg (4 lb) sugar

Prepare the fruits by picking over, hulling, etc., as necessary. Place the blackcurrants in a pan and barely cover with water. Bring to the boil and simmer until tender.

Add all the other fruits and simmer for a further 10 minutes. Add the sugar, stir to dissolve, then boil until setting point is reached. Pot into warm jars and cover.

Plum & Apple Jam

Windfall apples and the dark early plums are good for this jam.
Make as much as you can!

equal quantities of cooking apples and plums
water
sugar

Wash, peel, core and slice the apples. Put in a pan with a little water and boil until tender. Wash, halve and stone the plums and add to the apples. Continue cooking until the contents of the pan are soft and mushy. Rub through a sieve, then measure the purée. To every 600 ml (1 pint) purée add 350 g (12 oz) sugar.

Put the purée and sugar in a pan and bring to the boil, stirring to dissolve the sugar. Pot into warm jars and cover.

Green Tomato Jam

MAKES APPROX. 2 KG (4 LB)
1. 5 kg (3 lb) green tomatoes
1 kg (2 lb) cooking apples
2 lemons
25 g (1 oz) dried root ginger
water
1.5 kg (3 lb) sugar

Wash the tomatoes, cut into quarters. Peel and core the apples and cut into chunks. Put the tomatoes and apples in pan. Grate the rind from the lemons and squeeze the juice. Bruise the ginger and tie in a muslin bag. Add the lemon rind and juice and muslin bag to the pan with enough water to come to the level of the fruit. Bring to the boil and cook until the fruit is tender.

Add the sugar, stir until dissolved, then simmer, stirring occasionally, until thick. Remove the ginger. Pot into warm jars and cover.

Fig Jam

MAKES APPROX. 1.5 KG (3 LB)
1 kg (2 lb) dried figs
1 litre (2 pints) water
1.5 kg (3 lb) sugar
4 lemons

Wash the figs well and remove the stalks. Cut into 5–6 pieces, place in a bowl and cover with the water. Leave for 24 hours.

Next day, tip the figs and their soaking liquor into a pan. Bring to the boil, then add the sugar and stir until dissolved. Grate the rind from the lemons and squeeze the juice. Add the rind and juice to the pan and boil until setting point is reached. Pot into warm jars and cover.

Jellies

JELLY differs from jam in that all traces of pulp, skin or pips must be removed, but the main principles of jam-making apply to jelly.

Because only the juice is used in the making of a clear and sparkling jelly, considerably more fruit is needed than in jam-making. However, wild fruits from the hedgerows, such as blackberries, elderberries, bilberries and rowanberries, particularly when combined with apples, make delicious and economical jellies. Other fruits with a good pectin content are crab apples, quinces, black- and redcurrants, gooseberries

and damsons. Windfall and damaged fruit, if it is under-ripe, can be used for jelly-making providing all damaged parts are removed.

Jellies can be made from other fruits but so much extra pectin and acid have to be added to produce a good 'set' that the distinctive flavour of the fruit is often lost.

Herbs can be added to many fruits in jelly-making and the resulting jellies make delicious accompaniments to hot and cold meats and poultry.

Fruit juice added to the jelly will set varying amounts of sugar, from 350–500 g (12 oz–1 lb) per 600 ml (1 pint), depending on its pectin quality. It is therefore important to test for pectin in jelly-making.

Equipment

The equipment and tools suggested for jam-making (see page 10) are also suitable for jellies, with the addition of a jelly bag for straining the fruit. Jelly bags, with or without drip stands, can be bought, but a bag can easily be made at home from a square of cotton or flannel, or 6 layers of butter muslin. Always scald the cloth or bag thoroughly with boiling water before use.

For a homemade drip stand, tie each corner of the cloth to the legs of an upturned kitchen stool and place a bowl or basin underneath to catch the juice.

General Points

• Fruit used for jelly-making should be fresh and not over-ripe.

• Before cooking the fruit, wash it carefully, pick it over and discard any over-ripe fruit Cut away any unsound parts. It is not necessary to stalk currants, top and tail gooseberries, or peel apples.

• Just remove the larger leaves and stalks when washing the fruit.

• Always allow the pulp to drip in the jelly bag for up to 4 hours and, if possible, do not leave the juice longer than 24 hours before completing the jelly-making process. Prolonged standing will create a pectin breakdown and a darkening of colour.

- Never squeeze the jelly bag to hasten the process, as this will spoil the jelly by making it cloudy.

- The same tests for setting can be used for the jam: in general, the 'flake' test, or testing by temperature, will give the best results.

- Carry out the pectin test to ensure sufficient pectin is present. If not, place the juice in a clean pan and boil to reduce the volume.

- A good economical method of removing scum from jelly is to use a stainless steel perforated spoon. Dip it in boiling water and shake it before using it for skimming. The last bits of scum can be removed most easily by drawing a piece of greaseproof paper, with roughly torn edges, across the surface of the jelly.

- When scum has been removed, pot the jelly at once, as it will start setting in the pan.

- Ordinary jam jars are quite suitable for jellies, but smaller jars will aid setting. If they are an attractive shape, they make ideal presents, and can be put directly on the table. At one time, jellies were always potted in glass jars with slanting sides, so that the jelly could be turned out on a dish when required.

- When potting the jelly, pour it gently into a slightly tilted jar, as this helps to avoid bubbles forming.

- Place the disc, waxed side down, on the surface of the jelly as soon as you have filled the pots. Cellophane covers can be put on either at once, or when the jelly is cold and set. If you put them on at the same time as the disc, take care not to tilt or upset the jar, particularly if you want to enter it in a show or competition. Do not move jars until the jelly has set. Make certain the surface on which you place the jars is level.

- The storage points for jams also apply to jellies.

Note It is misleading to give approximate yields for each jelly recipe as results depend on the type and quality of the fruit used, and also on the growing season. Generally about 4.5 kg (10 lb) jelly will be obtained for every 3 kg (6 lb) used.

Loganberry & Redcurrant Jelly

1 kg (2 lb) redcurrants
1 kg (2 lb) loganberries
1 litre (2 pints) water
sugar

Wash the fruit. Drain well, then place in a pan with the water. Bring to the boil and simmer until fruit is soft. Tip into jelly bag to drip.

Measure the juice and test for pectin. To every 600 ml (1 pint) juice, add 500 g (1 lb) sugar. Put the juice and sugar in a saucepan and bring to the boil, stirring to dissolve the sugar. Boil hard until setting point is reached. Pot into warm jars and cover.

Damson Jelly

Try this jelly with a cream or cottage cheese.

3 kg (6 lb) damsons
water
sugar

Wash the damsons, discarding any that are green. Place in a pan and just cover with water. Simmer gently until the fruit is well broken down and pulpy – this will take about 45 minutes. Tip the pulp into a jelly bag and allow to drip for 2–3 hours.

Test for pectin. Measure the juice and add 500 g (1 lb) sugar to every 600 ml (1 pint) juice. Return to a clean pan. Stir well until the sugar has dissolved, then boil hard until setting point is reached. Pot into warm jars and cover.

Gooseberry & Elderflower Jelly

Elderflowers give a flavour to gooseberries which is similar
to muscatels.

2 kg (4 lb) gooseberries
water
sugar
3–4 sprays elderflower blossoms

Wash the gooseberries, place in a pan and barely cover with water.
Simmer gently until soft and pulpy, then tip the pulp into a jelly bag.
Allow to drip for 2–3 hours.

Test for pectin. Measure the juice and add 500 g (1 lb) sugar to every
600 ml (1 pint) juice. Return to a clean pan. Rinse the elderflower sprays
and wrap in a muslin bag. Put in the pan, making sure the bag is kept
below the surface of the juice during boiling. Bring to the boil, stirring
until the sugar has dissolved, and boil hard until setting point is reached.
Remove the elderflower blossoms. Pot the jelly into warm jars and cover.

Rose Hip Jelly

Use firm, just ripe rose hips. Windfall apples may be used,
provided any bruised or damaged portions are removed.

2 kg (4 lb) cooking apples
water
1 kg (2 lb) rose hips
sugar

Wash the apples, cut up and place in a pan with water to cover completely.
Bring to the boil and cook gently until soft and mushy.

Meanwhile, wash the rose hips and put through the coarse cut on a mincer. Add the minced rose hips to the pan and simmer gently for 10–15 minutes. Tip the pulp into a jelly bag and allow to drip overnight. Next day, measure the juice and test for pectin. To each 600 ml (1 pint) juice, add 500 g (1 lb) sugar. Put the juice and sugar in a pan and bring to the boil, stirring to dissolve the sugar. Boil until setting point is reached. Pot into warm jars and cover.

Crab Apple Jelly

3 kg (6 lb) crab apples
water
sugar

Wash the crab apples, paying particular attention to the blossom end, and remove the stalks. Place in a pan and cover with water, about 2 litres (4 pints). Simmer over gentle heat until completely tender and pulpy, then tip into a jelly bag and allow to drip.

Test for pectin. Measure the juice and return to a clean pan. Bring to boiling point. Add 500 g (1 lb) sugar to each 600 ml (1 pint) juice. Stir until the sugar has dissolved, then boil until setting point is reached. Pot into warm jars and cover.

Windfall Apples

If you use windfall apples instead of crab apples for your jelly, simmer a few loganberries, redcurrants or blackberries with them. This will greatly improve the colour, which can be poor with ordinary apples. A little dried root ginger or a few cloves will improve the flavour.

Redcurrant Jelly

3 kg (6 lb) redcurrants
water
sugar

Wash the redcurrants well, place in a pan and barely cover with water. Cook gently until really soft and pulpy, stirring occasionally. Tip the pulp into a jelly bag and allow to drip for 2–3 hours.

Test for pectin. Measure the juice and add 500 g (1 lb) sugar to every 600 ml (1 pint) juice. Return to a clean pan. Bring to the boil, stirring until the sugar has dissolved. Boil hard until setting point is reached. Pot into warm jars and cover.

Quick Mint Jelly

This is not a clear jelly, but the combined flavours of gooseberry and mint make it a little out of the ordinary. Do not enter it in a competition for a clear jelly. Sage jelly can be made in the same way, replacing mint with sage.

1 kg (2 lb) gooseberries
water
sugar
12 stalks fresh mint
few drops green food colouring

Wash the gooseberries, place in a pan and cover with cold water. Cook until really soft and pulpy, then push the pulp through a sieve, extracting as much juice as possible.

Test for pectin. Add 500 g (1 lb) sugar to each 600 ml (1 pint) juice and return to a clean pan. Wash and dry the mint in a bundle. Add to the pan and heat gently, stirring until the sugar has dissolved. Boil hard until setting point is reached. Remove the mint and add a few drops of green colouring. Pot the jelly into warm jars and cover.

Medlar Jelly

Delicious with cold meat, especially venison, this can also be served with scones and cream.

medlars
water
sugar
lemon juice

Wash the fruit well, weigh it and put it in a pan. Add 600 ml (1 pint) water to every 500 g (1 lb) fruit. Simmer slowly until the fruit is really soft and mushy. Tip into a jelly bag and leave to drip for several hours.

Test for pectin. Measure the juice and to each 600 ml (1 pint), add 350 g (12 oz) sugar and 1 x 15 ml spoon (1 tablespoon) lemon juice. Return to a clean pan. Bring slowly to the boil, stirring until the sugar has dissolved, then boil hard until setting point is reached. Pot into warm jars and cover.

Blackberry & Apple Jelly

2 kg (4 lb) blackberries
1 kg (2 lb) cooking apples
water
sugar

Rinse and drain the blackberries, wash and chop the apples and place both in a pan. Barely cover with water, then simmer gently until soft and mushy. Tip the pulp into a jelly bag and allow to drip for 2–3 hours.

Test for pectin. Measure the juice and add 500 g (1 lb) sugar to every 600 ml (1 pint) juice. Return to a clean pan. Stir until the sugar has dissolved, then boil hard until setting point is reached. Pot into warm jars and cover.

Tomato Jelly

This is good with salads and cold meats. It is not a clear jelly, so do not
enter it in a class for clear jelly at a show or competition.

MAKES APPROX. 2.5 KG (5 LB)
1. 5 kg (3 lb) ripe tomatoes
600 ml (1 pint) water
6 cloves
½ stick cinnamon
300 ml (½ pint) white vinegar
1.5 kg (3 lb) sugar
commercial pectin

Wash the tomatoes and place in a pan with the water. Wrap the spices
in a muslin or cotton bag and add to the pan. Cook gently until soft,
then remove the spice bag. Rub the pulp through a sieve. Return the
sieved pulp to the pan, add the vinegar and sugar and stir until the sugar
has dissolved. Add the pectin, in the quantities recommended by the
manufacturers. Boil rapidly until setting point is reached. Pot into warm
jars and cover.

Rowanberry Jelly (Mountain Ash)

rowanberries, or rowanberries and crab apples in equal quantities
water
sugar
lemons

Wash the berries well, and also the apples, if used. Just cover the fruit
with water and cook gently, stirring occasionally, until tender and mushy.
Tip into a jelly bag, and allow to drip for a few hours.

Measure the liquid and test for pectin. To each 600 ml (1 pint) juice, add 500 g (1 lb) sugar and the juice of a small lemon. (If crab apples are used, the lemon juice will not be needed.) Stir gently until the sugar has dissolved, then boil hard until setting point is reached. Pot into warm jars and cover.

Apple Jelly

Any windfalls or misshapen apples may be used for this jelly. Ordinary apple jelly can be rather flavourless, so add any of the following to give extra flavour: 12 whole cloves, 2 lumps dried root ginger, 12 stalks fresh mint.

3 kg (6 lb) cooking apples
water
sugar

Wash the apples, cutting out any bad bits. Cut into chunks and place in a pan. If using a flavouring, add to the pan. Root ginger should be well bruised with a hammer, and mint should be washed and drained. Cover the contents of the pan with water and cook gently until the apples are well broken down and mushy. Tip the pulp into a jelly bag and allow to drip for 4–5 hours.

Test for pectin. Measure the juice and add 500 g (1 lb) sugar to every 600 ml (1 pint) juice. Return to a clean pan. Stir until the sugar has dissolved, then boil hard until setting point is reached. Pot into warm jars and cover.

Two-in-one Recipe

Blackberry Jelly

blackberries
water
1 x 2.5 ml spoon (½ teaspoon) mixed spices
(grated nutmeg, ground mace, ground cinnamon)
to every 500 g (1 lb) fruit

Blackberry Cheese

lemons
sugar

Part 1: Pick over and wash the blackberries. Drain well and place in a pan. Barely cover with water and add the spices in the proportion given above. Bring to the boil and simmer until the fruit is soft and mushy. Tip the pulp into a jelly bag and allow to drip for 3–4 hours.

Test for pectin. Measure the juice and add 500 g (1 lb) sugar to every 600 ml (1 pint) juice. Return to a clean pan. Stir until the sugar has dissolved, then boil hard until setting point is reached. Pot into warm jars and cover.

Part 2: Remove the pulp from the jelly bag and rub through a fine wire or nylon sieve. Add 350 g (12 oz) sugar and the grated rind and juice of 1 small lemon to each 500 g (1 lb) of sieved pulp and place in a pan. Heat gently until the sugar has dissolved, then boil for 5–10 minutes, stirring constantly as the liquid evaporates. Pot into small warm jars and cover.

If possible, use containers of a shape suitable for the cheese to be turned out for serving. It is usually cut in slices and served with cold meats, but is equally good with toast and butter.

Green Gooseberry & Rhubarb Jelly

'Champagne' rhubarb has well-coloured red stems,
and is a good choice for use in jams and jellies.

3 kg (6 oz) green gooseberries
1 kg (2 oz) rhubarb
water
sugar

Top and tail the gooseberries, rinse if necessary and drain well. Trim the leaves and stalk ends from the rhubarb, wipe with a damp cloth and cut into chunks about 1 cm (½ in) long. Put together with the gooseberries in a pan, barely cover with water and cook gently, stirring occasionally, until the fruit is all tender. Tip into a jelly bag and allow to drip for a few hours.

Measure the juice, and test for pectin. Add 500 g (1 lb) sugar to every 600 ml (1 pint) juice. Bring to the boil, stirring until all the sugar has dissolved. Boil hard until setting point is reached. Pot into warm jars and cover.

Consistency of Cheeses

To check the consistency for cheeses, tilt the pan and draw a wooden spoon across the pulp. If no loose liquid oozes into the spoon's path, the consistency is correct and the cheese is ready for potting.

Apple & Sloe Jelly

This jelly goes very well with rabbit and hare.

equal quantities of green apples and ripe sloes
water
sugar

Rinse the apples and sloes and cut the apples into quarters if large. Put the fruit in a pan, cover with cold water and cook until soft and mushy. Tip the pulp into a jelly bag, and allow to drip for a few hours.

Measure the juice and test for pectin. To each 600 ml (1 pint) juice, add 500 g (1 lb) sugar. Bring to the boil, stirring until the sugar has dissolved. Then boil hard until setting point is reached. Pot into warm jars and cover.

Bramble Jelly

Very good with scones and cream.

blackberries
water
1 x 2.5 ml spoon (½ teaspoon) mixed spices to every 1 kg (2 lb) fruit
sugar

Pick over and wash the blackberries. Drain well, place in a pan and barely cover with water. Add the spices and bring to the boil. Simmer until soft and mushy. Tip into a jelly bag and allow to drip for a few hours.

Measure the juice. To every 600 ml (1 pint) juice, add 500 g (1 lb) sugar. Put the juice and sugar in a saucepan and bring to the boil, stirring to dissolve the sugar. Boil hard until setting point is reached. Pot into warm jars and cover.

Cranberry Jelly

If cranberries are expensive, use equal quantities of
cranberries and cooking apples.

1 kg (2 lb) cranberries
450 ml (¾ pint) water
sugar

Wash the cranberries. Place in a pan, add the water and bring to the boil.
Simmer until the skins have broken. Tip the pulp into a jelly bag and
allow to drip for a few hours.

Measure the juice. To each 600 ml (1 pint) add 500 g (1 lb) sugar.
Put the juice and sugar in a pan and bring to the boil, stirring to dissolve
the sugar. Boil until setting point is reached. Pot into warm jars and cover.

Marmalades

NOWADAYS, we think of marmalade as being made only from such citrus fruits as oranges, lemons, grapefruit and limes but, in the past, preserves made from other fruits were called 'marmalade'. You will occasionally find these recipes today, mostly using a combination of fruits – for example, apricot and orange marmalade.

There are two explanations given for the origin of the word 'marmalade'. The first suggests that it may have come from the Portuguese word for quince, which is *marmelo*. Older cookery books called quince preserves 'marmalade'. The second theory is perhaps more fanciful and stems from the voyage of Mary, Queen of Scots, from France to Scotland to claim her throne. She was very seasick, and one of her ladies, busy making a concoction of bitter oranges to relieve the sickness, said, '*Marie est malade*', which became shortened to 'marmalade'.

Most of our marmalade is made from bitter oranges, although these do not all come from Seville – at least half of our bitter oranges are from Malaga and Sicily. Shipments usually start to arrive here in mid to late December and continue until the third or fourth week of February.

Equipment

No additional equipment to that used for jams and jellies (see page 10) is required, other than a good sharp knife and a juice extractor.

General Points

• The principles of marmalade-making are much the same as for jam-making except that the thick peel of citrus fruits takes a longer time to cook and consequently more water is required.

• Most of the pectin, so necessary for a good 'set', is found in the pips and white inner skin or pith. For those who dislike pith in their marmalade, the peel can be removed from the pith and shredded finely. The pith should then be chopped roughly and put with the pips in a muslin bag. This is then cooked with the peel.

• Because the season for some citrus fruits, such as Sevilles, limes and tangerines, is short, they can be scrubbed, packed in suitable quantities and frozen until required.

• Remember to add extra fruit (one-eighth more than the normal recipe calls for) when using frozen fruit for marmalade to compensate for the pectin loss that occurs during frozen storage.

• Sliced peel and fruit can also be cooked and bottled for use later, in the same way as any other fruit. Be sure to make a note of the weight of the fruit on each bottle or packet to help when calculating the amount of sugar needed.

• Use fruit when it is fresh, before it has begun to shrivel and lose weight.

• Fruit should be well washed – a soft scrubbing brush is ideal for this.

• As in jam-making, the major part of the cooking is carried out before sugar is added. This usually takes 2–3 hours, unless a pressure cooker is used.

• If properly cooked, the peel should be soft enough to disintegrate between finger and thumb when squeezed.

• As with jam, the less boiling after the addition of sugar, the better the colour and flavour. Prolonged boiling darkens the colour, affects the flavour and the jelling properties begin to disappear.

- Add a nut of butter or a few drops of glycerine to the fruit and sugar mixture to reduce the amount of scum.

- Remove scum as soon as possible after setting point has been reached. If left much longer, it tends to cling to the pieces of peel.

- Allow marmalade to cool for 5–10 minutes, then stir gently before potting. This is to ensure even distribution of peel throughout the jar. (This is not necessary if twist tops are used, when the marmalade should be potted hot.)

Entering Marmalade for Show or Competition

If you like 'Old English' marmalade, and use either brown sugar or a little black treacle for flavour, do remember to state this on the label.

Whisky, rum, brandy or Grand Marnier can be added in the proportion of 1 x 15 ml spoon (1 tablespoon) to each jar just before potting. Again, remember to state this on the label.

Sweet oranges and lemons are frequently mixed with bitter oranges in a recipe. The pith of sweet oranges and lemons remains opaque after cooking, whereas with bitter oranges the pith becomes transparent. Therefore, if a clear appearance is required, you should remove the pith from sweet oranges and lemons and cook it with the pips.

Apricot & Orange Marmalade

If you intend to enter this marmalade for a show or competition,
check the schedule carefully to make sure the class is not
for citrus fruits only.

MAKES APPROX 2.5 KG (5 LB)
500 g (1 lb) dried apricots
2 oranges
1 lemon
1 litre (2 pints) water
1.5 kg (3 lb) sugar

Wash the apricots and put them in a bowl. Thinly slice the oranges and lemon (removing the pips and putting them in a muslin bag) and add to the apricots. Pour over the water. Allow to soak overnight.

Next day, tip the contents of the bowl into a pan and simmer until the peel is tender. Squeeze the bag of pips and remove from the pan. Add the sugar and stir until it has dissolved. Boil hard until setting point is reached. Pot into warm jars and cover.

Quick Ginger Marmalade

Use demerara or soft brown sugar, or a mixture of brown
and white sugar if you want to give this marmalade a darker
colour and fuller flavour.

MAKES APPROX. 2.5 KG (5 LB)
1 x 835 g (1 lb 13 oz) can unsweetened marmalade pulp
1.5 kg (3 lb) sugar
250 g (8 oz) preserved or crystallized ginger

Make the marmalade according to the directions on the can, but using 1.5 kg (3 lb) sugar. Finely chop the ginger and add after the sugar has dissolved. Pot into warm jars and cover.

Three-fruit Marmalade

MAKES APPROX. 4.5 KG (10 LB)
1.5 kg (3 lb) mixed fruit (lemons, grapefruit and sweet or bitter oranges)
3 litres (5 pints) water
3 kg (6 lb) sugar

Make in the same way as chunky Seville marmalade (see page 51), using any of the three cooking methods.

Lemon Jelly Marmalade

MAKES APPROX. 3 KG (6 LB)
1.5 kg (3 lb) lemons
3 litres (5 pints) water
sugar

Scrub the lemons and peel thinly. Shred the peel finely and tie in a muslin bag. Cut up the rest of the fruit roughly and place in a bowl, together with the muslin bag of peel. Pour on the water and leave to soak overnight.

Next day, tip the contents of the bowl into a pan and bring to the boil. Simmer for 1½–2 hours or until soft and tender.

Remove the muslin bag. Tip the fruit mixture into a jelly bag. Allow to drip for a few hours. Test for pectin, then measure the juice. To every 600 ml (1 pint) juice add 500 g (1 lb) sugar. Put the juice and sugar in a saucepan and add the muslin bag. Bring to the boil, stirring until the sugar has dissolved. Boil hard until setting point is reached. Remove the muslin bag, then pot into warm jars and cover.

Seville Orange Marmalade

MAKES APPROX. 4.5 KG (10 LB)
1. 5 kg (3 lb) Seville oranges
juice of 2 lemons or 1 x 5 ml spoon (1 teaspoon) citric or tartaric acid
3 litres (5 pints) water
3 kg (6 lb) sugar

Scrub the oranges, cut them in half and squeeze out the juice and pips. Slice or shred the fruit, or put it through the coarse cut of a mincer. (If you are intending to show or enter the marmalade for competition, do not mince the fruit.) Put the fruit, orange juice, lemon juice or acid and water in a pan with the orange pips tied in a muslin bag. Cook gently for 2 hours or until the peel is really soft.

Squeeze the bag of pips and remove. Test for pectin. Add the sugar and stir until it has dissolved. Bring to the boil and boil hard until setting point is reached. Cool, stir gently, pot into warm jars and cover. If using jars with twist tops, pot the marmalade while still hot.

Chunky Seville Marmalade

MAKES APPROX. 4.5 KG (10 LB)
1.5 kg (3 lb) Seville oranges
3 litres (5 pints) water
juice of 2 lemons, or 2 x 5 ml spoons (2 teaspoons) citric or tartaric acid
3 kg (6 lb) sugar

Scrub the oranges and cook them whole, with the water and lemon juice or acid:
• in a covered casserole in a slow oven (160°C, 325°F/Gas 3) for 4–5 hours; *or*
• in a covered saucepan on top of the stove for 2 ½ –3 hours; *or*
• in a pressure cooker at high pressure (7-kg/15-lb) for 20 minutes, using *half* the quantity of water. Allow the pressure cooker to cool for 10 minutes at room temperature before opening. This is important as it is part of the cooking time.

When the peel is soft, remove the fruit from the liquid and chop it roughly. This can be done easily with a knife and fork or a pair of scissors. Separate the pips from the cut-up fruit and return them to the liquid in the pan. Boil hard for 5–6 minutes. Strain the liquid into a preserving pan and add the fruit and sugar. Stir until the sugar has dissolved. Boil hard until setting point is reached. After cooling (stirring occasionally) pot into warm jars and cover. For twist-top jars, pot while still hot.

Jelly Marmalade

Lemons can be substituted for oranges in this recipe.

MAKES APPROX. 2.5 KG (5 LB)
1 kg (2 lb) Seville oranges
2 litres (4 pints) water
juice of 2 lemons
1.5 kg (3 lb) sugar

Scrub the oranges. Peel the rind thinly from half of the oranges and shred finely. Place the rind in a pan, add enough water to cover and cook gently, covered, until tender.

Meanwhile, cut up the fruit, add the remainder of the water and the lemon juice and cook, covered, in another pan for 2 hours, or until tender and pulpy. Strain the liquid from the shredded orange rind (reserving the rind) and tip into a jelly bag. Leave to drip for 1 hour.

Test for pectin. Put the liquid and shredded rind in a preserving pan. Simmer for 10 minutes, then add the sugar. Stir until the sugar has dissolved, then boil hard until setting point is reached. Allow the marmalade to cool for a few minutes (unless using twist tops) before potting to distribute the shreds evenly. Pot into warm jars and cover.

Grapefruit Marmalade

MAKES APPROX. 3–3.5 KG (6–7 LB)
1. 5 kg (3 lb) grapefruit
3 litres (5 pints) water
3 kg (6 lb) sugar
2 x 5 ml spoons (2 teaspoons) citric or tartaric acid

Scrub the fruit well. Cut in half, then slice, preferably on a plate to catch the juice. Remove the pips and place in a muslin bag. Put the sliced fruit, together with any juice, and the bag of pips in a pan. Add the water and bring to the boil. Cook gently for 2 hours, or until the peel is tender.

Remove the bag of pips after squeezing against the side of the pan. Add the sugar and citric or tartaric acid. Stir until dissolved, then boil hard until setting point is reached. Pot into warm jars and cover.

Grapefruit Marmalade

The zest of the fruit will give an opaque appearance to the finished marmalade. This variety is not a good one to enter for competitions but it is still delicious for family use!

Oxford Marmalade

MAKES APPROX. 6 KG (13 LB)
2 kg (4 lb) Seville oranges
2 lemons
5 litres (9 pints) water
2 kg (4 lb) white sugar
2 kg (4 lb) brown sugar

Scrub the fruit and cut into bite-size chunks. Collect all pips and juice, and put the pips and any pith that may have been removed into a muslin bag. Put the cut-up fruit, juice and bag of pips in a pan and cover with the water. Leave overnight.

Next day, bring to the boil and simmer gently until the peel is tender and the contents of the pan almost halved. Test for pectin. Add the sugars and stir until dissolved. Boil hard until setting point is reached. Remove the pips, then pot into warm jars and cover

Tangerine Marmalade

MAKES APPROX. 2.5–3 KG (5–6 LB)
1 kg (2 lb) tangerines
1 grapefruit and 1 lemon, combined weight
approx. 350 g (12 oz)
1 x 2.5 ml spoon (½ teaspoon) tartaric acid
2. 7 litres (4½ pints) water
1.5 kg (3 lb) sugar

Scrub the fruit. Remove the peel from the tangerines and shred. Tie the shreds in a muslin bag. Peel the grapefruit and lemon and put the peel through a mincer. Cut up all the fruit and place in a pan with the minced peel and muslin bag of shredded peel. Add the tartaric acid and water and bring to the boil.

Cook gently for 2 hours, removing the bag of tangerine peel after 40 minutes. Tip the tangerine peel out of the bag into a sieve or colander and rinse under a cold tap and leave in cold water. Tip the fruit pulp into a jelly bag and allow to drip for a few hours. Test for pectin.

Return the juice to a clean pan, add the sugar and the cooked shreds. Warm the mixture sufficiently to dissolve the sugar, stirring all the time. Boil the marmalade hard until setting point is reached. Pot into warm jars and cover.

Quick Four-fruit Marmalade

MAKES APPROX. 3 KG (6 LB)
2 grapefruit
2 lemons
2 Seville or sweet oranges
2 tangerines or limes
water
sugar

Scrub the fruit and cut into quarters. Remove the pips, put in a small bowl and cover with water. Put the fruit in a separate bowl and just cover with water. Leave both bowls overnight.

Next day, place the fruit and soaking water in a pan and bring to the boil. Cook until tender. Remove the fruit from the liquid and cut into small chunks, according to your taste. Return the fruit to the pan of liquid and add the strained liquid from the pips.

Measure the contents of the pan, and to every 600 ml (1 pint), add 500 g (1 lb) sugar. Bring to the boil, stirring until the sugar has dissolved. Boil hard until setting point is reached. Pot into warm jars and cover.

Curds

CURDS are sometimes confused with butters and cheeses. A fruit butter is soft and spreadable; a cheese is thicker and should be turned out and sliced for serving; and a curd is usually fairly rich and generally contains eggs and butter.

Curds do not normally keep long because the egg content means they cannot be brought to boiling point or they would curdle. For this reason, they are not regarded as a true preserve in shows and competitions and, unless specifically included on the schedule, should not be entered.

Lemon is the classic curd but other fruits, such as oranges, apples, apricots and gooseberries can also be used and it is well worth experimenting with a mixture of fruits.

Generally, the fruits used for jellies are also the best ones for butters and cheeses, which is why they are often made from the pulp left in the jelly bag, after the juice has dripped. Butters and cheeses are also useful for using up a glut.

Equipment

As for jams (see page 10), with the addition of a double saucepan. This is not absolutely essential, but very useful, as slow gentle cooking is necessary to make curds. A heatproof bowl, placed over a pan of hot water, can be used as a substitute.

Small jars are preferable because, once opened, curds do not keep as long as jams, etc. Smaller jars can also be placed straight on the table. Do not use twist tops, pliable plastic tops or plastic film to cover curds as they encourage mould.

General Points

•   Do not overbeat the eggs before adding to the mixture: this can result in bubbles in the finished curd.

•   Strain in the beaten eggs to ensure that there are no lumps of egg white in the curd.

•   Cook the curd gently, stirring to prevent it sticking to the pan. As the amount of juice from lemons varies, if, at end of the cooking time, the curd seems very thin, add another egg yolk and cook for a further 5–10 minutes. Remember that curd will thicken considerably as it cools. It will also shrink considerably in the jar, so fill the jars right up to the brim.

•   Do not use 'farmhouse' or salty butters when making curds, as this affects the delicate flavour.

Lemon Curd

Orange curd can be made following this recipe, using three sweet oranges and one lemon.

MAKES APPROX. 750 G–1 KG (1½–2 LB)
3 large or 4 medium-sized lemons
250 g (8 oz) butter
500 g (1 lb) sugar
5 eggs

Scrub the lemons. Grate the rind on fine side of a grater and squeeze out the juice. Place the rind, juice, butter and sugar in the top part of a double saucepan over hot water on low heat. Allow to melt slowly, stirring occasionally. When the sugar has dissolved, strain in the beaten eggs. Cook gently, stirring occasionally, until the curd coats the back of a spoon. Pot into warm jars and cover with transparent cellulose and wax discs. Use within 6 weeks, or 3 months if kept in the refrigerator.

Marrow & Lemon Curd

A good filling for tarts and flans, this will keep up to 4 months.
An ordinary saucepan can be used for this recipe, provided
it is kept over a very gentle heat, and is attended
right through the cooking process.

MAKES APPROX. 2–3 KG (4–6 LB)
2 kg (4 lb) prepared marrow
1.7 kg (3½ lb) sugar
250 g (8 oz) butter
6 lemons
2 eggs

Peel the marrow and discard the seeds. Cut into cubes or chunks and steam until very tender. Drain very thoroughly, then mash or liquidize until smooth. Return to the pan and add the sugar and butter. Grate the lemon rind and squeeze the juice. Add to the pan. Heat gently, stirring until the butter and sugar have completely dissolved. Simmer very gently for a further 30 minutes, stirring constantly as the mixture thickens. Do not let it boil (it may curdle). Pot into warm jars and cover.

Eggs for Lemon Curd

Try to use eggs with deep-coloured yolks, as this will produce a beautiful, rich-looking curd.

Apple Curd

This is good as a spread or cake filling, or as a filling for tartlets.

MAKES APPROX. 1.25 KG (2½ LB)
1 kg (2 lb) cooking apples
500 g (1 lb) sugar
250 g (8 oz) butter
1 x 5 ml spoon (1 teaspoon) ground cinnamon
or 2 x 5 ml spoons (2 teaspoons) ground ginger
2 eggs

Peel and core the apples and cook in a minimum of water until mushy. Place in the top of a double saucepan with the sugar, butter and spices. Stir over hot water on low heat until the butter and sugar are dissolved. Strain in the beaten eggs. Continue cooking over moderate heat until thick. Pot into warm jars and cover.

Apricot Curd

MAKES APPROX. 500 G (1 LB)
175 g (6 oz) dried apricots
250 g (8 oz) sugar
50 g (2 oz) butter
1 lemon
2 eggs

Wash the apricots, cover with water and let soak 24 hours. Cook gently until tender. Put through a coarse sieve or liquidize. Put the apricot pulp in the top of a double saucepan and add the sugar and butter. Grate the lemon rind and squeeze the juice. Add to the pan and place over hot water. Cook gently over low heat, stirring until the butter and sugar are dissolved. Strain the beaten eggs into the pan and continue cooking until the mixture thickens to coat the back of a spoon. Pot into warm jars and cover.

Gooseberry Curd

MAKES APPROX. 1.5 KG (3 LB)
1.5 kg (3 lb) gooseberries
600 ml (1 pint) water
750 g (1½ lb) sugar
125 g (4 oz) butter
4 eggs

Wash the gooseberries, top and tail them and put in a pan with the water. Simmer until they are soft and pulpy. Rub through a coarse sieve to remove the seeds, then put the pulp in the top of a double saucepan. Add the sugar and butter and put over hot water. Cook gently over low heat, stirring until the butter and sugar are dissolved. Strain in the beaten eggs and continue cooking gently, stirring, until the mixture thickens and will coat the back of the spoon. Pot into warm jars and cover.

Honey Curd

MAKES APPROX. 1 KG (2 LB)
600 ml (1 pint) clear honey
grated rind of 2 lemons
juice of 4 lemons
125 g (4 oz) butter
4 eggs plus 2 extra yolks

Strain the honey, then place in the top of a double saucepan with the lemon rind and juice and the butter. Place over hot water on low heat. Allow to melt, stirring, occasionally. Beat together the egg yolks and whites and strain into the pan. Continue cooking over low heat, stirring occasionally, until the mixture thickens and will coat the back of a spoon. Pot into warm jars and cover.

Chutneys, Relishes, Sauces & Vinegars

Chutneys

CHUTNEYS are made from fruit or vegetables, or a mixture of the two, with vinegar, salt and spices acting as preserving agents. There is plenty of scope for individual tastes and ideas in combining different ingredients and spices. Such fruits as windfall apples, green tomatoes and end-of-season sticks of rhubarb can be used because there is no worry about the setting qualities of chutney ingredients. But remember, as with any new recipe, make only a small quantity of a chutney at first, to see if the family approves.

A good chutney should be of a reasonably smooth texture, almost jam-like and it should have a mellow flavour. Slow, gentle cooking gives the characteristic smooth texture and helps to extract and blend the different flavours. The finished chutney mellows with keeping and, unless otherwise stated in a recipe, should be kept for at least 6–8 weeks before eating.

Chutneys are an invaluable part of the store cupboard. They will add interest and flavour to so many dishes, from curries to grilled fish and kedgeree, from casseroles to cold meat and poultry salads and to bread and cheese snacks.

Vinegar

Use a good-quality vinegar with an acetic acid content of at least 5 per cent. White vinegar will give a lighter colour to the chutney, but some people think malt vinegar gives a better flavour. (Remember, however, that the depth of colour is no indication of the strength of the vinegar.)

Equipment

Never use metal spoons, knives or forks in making chutney because they can give it an unpleasant metallic taste.

Saucepans Aluminium, stainless steel or enamel-lined.

Sieves Stainless steel or nylon.

Muslin or cotton squares Use to tie up whole spices wanted for flavourings.

Scales Dual markings, metric and imperial.

Spoons Long-handled, wooden.

Mincer Not essential but can save time.

Chopping board and stainless steel knife.

Jars Assorted shapes and sizes.

Covers Vinegar corrodes metal, so use plastic screw or snap-on tops or plastic preserving skin. Metal tops, if used, must be lined or coated with plastic (you will find that twist tops on modern jam jars are so lined). Squares of cotton material dipped in paraffin wax and tied down tightly may also be used.

General Points

• Apples, gooseberries, plums, ripe tomatoes, green tomatoes, rhubarb, marrow and beetroot are all good bases for chutney, so take advantage of any glut or cheap offers. Brown sugar gives a better colour to chutney than other types of sugar. Alternatively, use granulated sugar and add a little black treacle.

• It is best to use whole spices in chutney-making. These should be gently bruised, tied in a muslin bag and cooked with the other ingredients.

• They are preferable to ground spices, which can give a muddy appearance to the finished chutney. Sometimes, however, a recipe requires a mixture of whole and ground spices to give the best flavour. Cinnamon, allspice, nutmeg, mace, cloves and coriander are sweet aromatic spices. Ginger, mustard, cayenne pepper and curry powder are 'hot' spices.

• If chutney has shrunk in the jar, the cover is not airtight and moisture has evaporated.

• If loose liquid has collected on top of the chutney, it has not been cooked sufficiently. You maybe able to rescue it by bringing it to the boil again and cooking until the liquid disappears.

• Where tough or fibrous fruit and vegetables, such as onions, apples and gooseberries are included in a recipe, it is a good idea to soften them first in a small amount of water in a closed pan. The remainder of the cooking should be done in an open pan, as evaporation of liquid is an important part of the cooking process, but the cooking should be long and slow to produce a smooth, 'jam-like' consistency.

• To test whether chutney has reached the required consistency, draw a wooden spoon through the mixture: it should leave a clean path with no free liquid showing.

• The variety of spices and dried fruit in a recipe may be changed, but keep the proportions of fruit, vegetables, sugar and vinegar the same to ensure the correct consistency.

Spiced Vinegar

Ready-spiced vinegars can be bought but they are easy to make and offer opportunities for individual tastes. They are at their best if whole spices are allowed to steep in the unheated vinegar for 6–8 weeks. Add 25 g (1 oz) of whole mixed pickling spices to a 1-litre (2-pint) bottle of vinegar. Remove a little of the vinegar to make space for the spices. Screw the top back on and leave the bottle to stand for the 6–8 weeks. During this time, the spices will gradually sink to the bottom of the bottle. Strain before use.

If spiced vinegar is required for use at short notice, put the vinegar and pickling spices in a basin or bowl and stand the bowl over a saucepan of water. Cover the basin with a plate, otherwise much of the flavour will be lost. Bring the water in the saucepan to boiling point, then draw the pan off the heat and allow the pickling spices to steep in the warm vinegar for 2 hours. Strain, cool and use as required.

Green Tomato Chutney

MAKES APPROX. 3. 5 KG (7 LB)
2 kg (4 lb) green tomatoes
750 g (1½ lb) shallots
500 g (1lb) cooking apples
600 ml (1 pint) vinegar
250 g (8 oz) seedless raisins or dates
12 red chillies
25 g (1 oz) dried root ginger
2 x 5 ml spoons (2 teaspoons) salt
500 g (1lb) sugar

Wash and finely chop the tomatoes. Peel and chop the shallots. Peel, core and chop the apples. Put the tomatoes, shallots and apples in a pan and add half the vinegar. If using dates, stone and chop them. Bruise the chillies and ginger and tie in a muslin bag. Add the raisins or dates and spice bag to the pan and cook until soft and pulpy. Add the remaining vinegar, the salt and sugar and stir well. Continue cooking until thick, pressing the bag of spices occasionally with the wooden spoon. Remove the bag, pot into warm jars and cover.

Chutneys for Competitions

All chutneys entered for show or competition should be in clear glass jars, suitable for chutney (e.g. not fish paste jars). There should be no proprietary brand mark on the jar and all jars should be labelled with the date of making and the variety of chutney, stating whether it is mild or hot.

Rhubarb Chutney

If you prefer, you could replace half the rhubarb with apples.

MAKES APPROX. 2.5 KG (5 LB)
2 kg (4 lb) rhubarb
500 g (1 lb) onions
250 g (8 oz) dates
1 litre (2 pints) vinegar
2 x 15 ml spoons (2 tablespoons) ground mixed spice
2 x 5 ml spoons (2 teaspoons) ground ginger or curry powder
25 g (1 oz) salt
1 kg (2 lb) sugar

Wipe the rhubarb and cut into chunks. Peel and mince or chop the onions. Stone and chop the dates. Put these ingredients in a pan with half the vinegar and cook slowly until tender. Add the spices, salt, sugar and remainder of the vinegar and stir well. Simmer gently until thick. Pot into warm jars and cover.

Beetroot Chutney

MAKES APPROX. 2.5 KG (5 LB)
1.5 kg (3 lb) beetroot
500 g (1 lb) onions
1 litre (2 pints) vinegar
500 g (1 lb) cooking apples
500 g (1 lb) seedless raisins or dates
3 x 15 ml spoons (3 tablespoons) ground ginger
1 x 5 ml spoon (1 teaspoon) salt
1 kg (2 lb) sugar

Wash the beetroot and cook in water to cover until tender. Drain and allow to cool, then peel and cut into cubes. (Alternatively, if a smooth chutney is preferred, mash well.) Peel and chop the onions and put in a pan with a little of the vinegar. Cook gently until soft.

Peel, core and chop the apples and add to the pan. If using dates, stone and chop them. Add the raisins or dates to the pan and continue cooking until pulpy. Add the cooked beetroot, ginger, salt and half the remaining vinegar. Simmer gently until thick. Stir in the sugar and remaining vinegar and continue cooking until thick again. Pot into warm jars and cover.

Turnip Chutney

MAKES APPROX. 2 KG (4 LB)
1 kg (2 lb) turnips
500 g (1 lb) apples
500 g (1 lb) onions
250 g (8 oz) sultanas or dates
250 g (8 oz) sugar
12 g (½ oz) turmeric
1 x 5 ml spoon (1 teaspoon) dry mustard
25 g (1 oz) salt
pinch cayenne or black pepper
600 ml (1 pint) vinegar

Peel and chop the turnips. Cook in gently boiling water until tender. Drain and mash, then put in a clean pan. Peel, core and chop the apples. Peel and chop the onions. If using dates, stone and chop them. Add the apples, onions, sultanas or dates and sugar to the pan and stir well. Mix the turmeric, mustard, salt and pepper together with a little of the vinegar, add to the pan and mix well. Add the remainder of the vinegar, and bring to the boil, stirring occasionally. Cook gently until thick. Pot into hot jars and seal. Ready for use in 4–6 weeks.

Plum Chutney

The flavour of plums in this recipe blends well with cold beef.

MAKES APPROX. 2.5 KG (5 LB)

1 kg (2 lb) plums (or damsons, if preferred)
500 g (1 lb) onions
500 g (1 lb) apples
600 ml (1 pint) vinegar
500 g (1 lb) seedless raisins or dates
1 x 15 ml spoon (1 tablespoon) salt
1 x 5 ml spoon (1 teaspoon) ground ginger
1 x 5 ml spoon (1 teaspoon) ground allspice
pinch grated nutmeg
pinch ground cloves
500 g (1 lb) sugar

Wash and stone the plums. (If using damsons, it is best to remove the stones as they rise to the surface during cooking.) Peel and chop the onions. Peel, core and chop the apples. Place these ingredients in a pan, add half the vinegar and cook until soft. If using dates, stone and chop them. Add the raisins or dates, salt and spices and continue cooking until thick. Stir in the sugar with the remainder of the vinegar and continue to simmer gently until the mixture thickens again. Pot into warm jars and cover.

Blackberry & Apple Chutney (Seedless)

A mild chutney that goes well with all cold meats.

MAKES APPROX. 2.5 KG (5 LB)
1 kg (2 lb) cooking apples
500 g (1 lb) onions
3 kg (6 lb) blackberries
1 litre (2 pints) vinegar
1 x 15 ml spoon (1 tablespoon) grated nutmeg
1 x 15 ml spoon (1 tablespoon) ground allspice
1 x 5 ml spoon (1 teaspoon) cayenne pepper
2 x 5 ml (2 teaspoons) salt
1 kg (2 lb) sugar

Wash and chop the apples, without peeling, and peel and finely chop or mince the onions. Put both of these in a pan with the washed and drained blackberries. Add 300 ml (½ pint) of the vinegar and cook slowly until the fruit and onions are soft and pulped. Rub the pulp through a sieve and return the purée to a clean pan. Add the spices, salt and half the remaining vinegar. Cook gently, then add the sugar and the rest of the vinegar. Stir well and continue cooking until thick, stirring frequently. Pot into warm jars and cover.

Date Chutney

MAKES APPROX. 1 KG (2 LB)
500 g (1 lb) dates
125 g (4 oz) onions
125 g (4 oz) seedless raisins
125 g (4 oz) walnuts or hazelnuts
1 x 5 ml spoon (1 teaspoon) ground mixed spice
pinch cayenne pepper
1 x 2.5 ml spoon (½ teaspoon) salt or garlic salt
600 ml (1 pint) white or cider vinegar
125 g (4 oz) sugar

Stone and mince or finely chop the dates. Peel and mince or finely chop the onions. Mince or finely chop the raisins and nuts. Place all these ingredients in a pan with the spices, salt and vinegar. Bring to the boil and cook gently until tender, stirring occasionally. Add the sugar and stir to dissolve. Continue cooking until thick, stirring occasionally. Pot into warm jars and cover.

Apple & Walnut Chutney

A 'nutty' chutney that makes a good accompaniment,
to cold pork. It is also ideal for topping small biscuit
and cheese cocktail snacks.

1 kg (2 lb) cooking apples
2 oranges
1 lemon
75 g (3 oz) walnuts
250 g (8 oz) sultanas or raisins
500 g (1 lb) soft brown sugar
450 ml (¾ pint) spiced vinegar

Peel, core and chop the apples. Grate the rind from the oranges and lemon, then squeeze out the juice. Put the rind and juice in a saucepan with the apples. Chop the walnuts and add with the remaining ingredients. Stir and bring slowly to the boil.

Cook gently until thick, stirring occasionally. Pot into warm jars and cover.

Date & Apple Chutney

This is a mild, sweet chutney. If the apples are not very juicy, increase the vinegar by 150 ml (¼ pint).

MAKES APPROX. 1.5–1.7 KG (3–3½ LB)

500 g (1 lb) onions
water
1 kg (2 lb) cooking apples
1 kg (2 lb) dates
600 ml (1 pint) vinegar
1 x 5 ml spoon (1 teaspoon) salt
1 x 5 ml spoon (1 teaspoon) ground ginger
1 x 5 ml spoon (1 teaspoon) dry mustard
1 x 2.5 ml spoon (½ teaspoon) cayenne pepper
250 g (8 oz) sugar

Peel and chop or mince the onions and put in a pan with a little water. Cook gently until soft. Peel, core and chop the apples. Stone and chop the dates. Add the apples and dates to the pan with half the vinegar, the salt, ginger, mustard and cayenne. Cook until thick, stirring occasionally.

Add the sugar and the remainder of the vinegar. Stir well and continue cooking until thick, stirring occasionally. Pot into warm jars and cover.

Mint Chutney

MAKES APPROX. 1 KG (2 LB)
1 kg (2 lb) cooking apples
250 g (8 oz) seedless raisins
450 ml (¾ pint) spiced vinegar (see page 66)
150 g (5 oz) sugar
1 x 15 ml spoon (1 teaspoon) salt
1 x 2.5 ml spoon (½ teaspoon) cayenne pepper
25–50 g (1–2 oz) fresh mint

Peel and core the apples. Put the apples and raisins through the coarse cut on a mincer. Place in a pan with the vinegar, sugar, salt and cayenne and bring to the boil, stirring to dissolve the sugar. Cook gently for 30 minutes.

Wash the mint, drain well, then chop and add to the pan. Continue cooking until thick, stirring occasionally. Pot into warm jars and cover.

Mango Chutney

This is one of the classic chutneys to serve with curry.
It goes well with all spicy rice dishes, such as pilau.

MAKES APPROX. 750 G (1½ LB)
500 g (1 lb) mangoes, fresh or canned
250 g (8 oz) cooking apples
1 x 2.5 ml spoon (½ teaspoon) salt
175 g (6 oz) onions
600 ml (1 pint) spiced vinegar (see page 66)
1 x 5 ml spoon (1 teaspoon) ground ginger
300 g (10 oz) brown sugar

Peel and slice the mangoes if they are fresh; drain if they are canned. Peel, core and slice the apples and put in a bowl with the mangoes. Sprinkle with the salt and leave overnight.

Next day, rinse and drain mangoes and apples. Peel and finely chop the onions and put in a saucepan with the mangoes, apples, vinegar and ginger. Bring to the boil and simmer gently until the fruit and onions are soft. Add the sugar and stir until it has dissolved. Continue simmering, stirring occasionally, until the chutney is very thick. Pot into warm jars and seal.

Apple Chutney

This is a good basic chutney that goes well with anything.

MAKES APPROX. 3 KG (6 LB)
1 kg (2 lb) onions
water
2 kg (4 lb) cooking apples
4 cloves garlic (optional)
500 g (1 lb) sultanas or dates
1 litre (2 pints) vinegar
1 x 15 ml spoon (1 tablespoon) ground cinnamon
1 x 15 ml spoon (1 tablespoon) ground ginger
1 x 5 ml spoon (1 teaspoon) cayenne
1 x 15 ml spoon (1 tablespoon) salt
1 kg (2 lb) sugar

Peel and chop the onions and put in a pan with a little water. Cook slowly until soft. Peel, core and chop the apples. Crush the garlic, if used. If using dates, stone and chop them. Add the apples and garlic to the pan with half the vinegar, the sultanas or dates and the spices. Cook slowly until pulpy. Add the salt, sugar and remaining vinegar and continue cooking until the chutney is thick, stirring occasionally. Pot into warm jars and cover.

Elderberry Chutney

If you prefer, you can replace the garlic with 250 g (8 oz) onions in this chutney. Peel, chop them finely and add to the pan with the elderberries and apples.

MAKES APPROX. 1.7 KG (3½ LB)
500 g (1 lb) elderberries
500 g (1 lb) cooking apples
250 g (8 oz) seedless raisins
900 ml (1½ pints) vinegar
75 g (3 oz) dried root ginger
1 x 15 ml spoon (1 tablespoon) mustard seed
3–4 dried chillies
25 g (1 oz) garlic
1 x 5 ml spoon (1 teaspoon) salt
1 kg (2 lb) sugar

Wash the elderberries. Peel, core and chop the apples. Place the berries and apples in a pan and add the raisins and vinegar. Bruise the root ginger well and tie in muslin with the mustard seed and chillies. Add to the pan and bring to the boil. Cook gently until the fruit is tender.

Crush the garlic with the salt and add to the pan with the sugar. Stir until the sugar has dissolved, then cook gently until thick. Remove the bag of spices. Pot into warm jars and cover.

Pear Chutney

If hard cooking pears are used in this recipe, it is advisable to cook them for 30 minutes in a very little water to soften them before adding to the other ingredients. This is a good chutney to serve with poultry.

MAKES APPROX. 1.5 KG (3 LB)
1 kg (2 lb) pears
250 g (8 oz) onions
250 g (8 oz) tomatoes (green or red)
125 g (4 oz) dates or seedless raisins
250 g (8 oz) celery
600 ml (1 pint) vinegar
1 x 2.5 ml spoon (½ teaspoon) cayenne pepper
1 x 2.5 ml spoon (½ teaspoon) ground ginger
1 x 5 ml spoon (1 teaspoon) salt
350 g (12 oz) soft brown sugar

Peel, core and chop the pears. Peel and chop the onions. Wash and slice the tomatoes. Stone and chop the dates or chop the raisins. Wash, dry and chop the celery. Place all these ingredients in a pan and add the vinegar and spices. Bring to the boil and simmer gently until tender, stirring occasionally.

Add the salt and sugar and stir until dissolved. Continue cooking until thick, stirring occasionally. Pot into warm jars and cover.

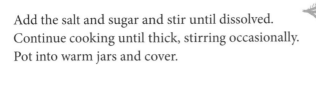

Marrow or Pumpkin Chutney

MAKES APPROX. 2 KG (4 LB)
1. 5 kg (3 lb) marrow or pumpkin
500 g (1 lb) onions
500 g (1 lb) ripe tomatoes
600 ml (1 pint) vinegar
125 g (4 oz) sultanas or dates
2 x 5 ml spoons (2 teaspoons) allspice
2 x 5 ml spoons (2 teaspoons) ground ginger
2 x 15 ml spoons (2 tablespoons) salt
2 x 5 ml spoons (2 teaspoons) black pepper
750 g (1½ lb) brown sugar

Peel the marrow or pumpkin and cut into small chunks. Peel and chop or mince the onions. Peel and slice the tomatoes. Put all these ingredients in a pan with half the vinegar. If using dates, stone and chop them and add these or the sultanas to the pan. Simmer gently until soft and pulpy and the marrow can be easily crushed.

Add spices, pepper and salt and simmer for a further 15 minutes. Stir in the sugar and remaining vinegar. Continue cooking until thick. Pot into warm jars and cover.

Marrow Chutney

The mild flavour of this chutney blends well with cream cheese.

MAKES APPROX. 2 KG (4 LB)
1.5 kg (3 lb) marrow
salt
350 g (12 oz) cooking apples
250 g (8 oz) onions
250 g (8 oz) sultanas or dates
900 ml (1½ pints) vinegar
25 g (1 oz) dried root ginger
12–18 peppercorns
175 g (6 oz) sugar

Peel, seed and chop the marrow into small cubes. Sprinkle with salt and leave overnight. Next day rinse and drain the marrow and place in a pan.

Peel, core and chop the apples. Peel and chop the onions. If using dates, stone and chop them, or chop the sultanas. Add the apples, onions, dates or sultanas and vinegar to the pan. Bruise the ginger and tie with the peppercorns in a muslin bag. Add to the pan. Bring to the boil, stirring occasionally, then simmer until tender.

Add the sugar and stir until dissolved. Continue cooking until thick, stirring occasionally. Remove the muslin bag, then pot into warm jars and cover.

Orange Chutney

This is delicious with duck or game.

MAKES APPROX. 2.5 KG (5 LB)
500 g (1 lb) onions
water
1 kg (2 lb) cooking apples
2 kg (4 lb) sweet oranges
500 g (1 lb) sultanas or seedless raisins
1 x 15 ml spoon (1 tablespoon) salt
2 x 5 ml spoons (2 teaspoons) ground ginger
2 x 5 ml spoons (2 teaspoons) cayenne pepper
2 litres (4 pints) vinegar
1 kg (2 lb) sugar

Peel and chop the onions and put in a pan with a little water. Cook gently until soft. Peel, core and chop the apples and add to the pan. Continue cooking gently. Scrub the oranges, then peel, removing as much white pith as possible. Put the peel and pulp through a mincer, being careful not to lose any of the juice. Add the minced oranges, sultanas or raisins, salt, spices and half the vinegar to the pan.

Simmer gently for about 1 hour or until thick and the orange peel is tender. Add the sugar and remaining vinegar and continue simmering until the mixture is thick again. Pot into warm jars and cover. Store for 6 weeks before using.

Apricot Chutney

A good fruity chutney for poultry, particularly duck.

MAKES APPROX. 1 KG (2 LB)
250 g (8 oz) dried apricots
125 g (4 oz) seedless raisins or dates
500 g (1 lb) cooking apples
1 lemon
125 g (4 oz) sultanas
1 x 5 ml spoon (1 teaspoon) salt
600 ml (1 pint) vinegar
2 x 5 ml (2 teaspoons) whole mixed pickling spices
500 g (1 lb) sugar

Wash and finely chop the apricots. Cover with water and soak for 4–5 hours, or overnight, if convenient. Drain and put in a pan. If using dates, stone and chop them. Peel, core and chop the apples. Grate the lemon rind and squeeze the juice. Add the raisins or dates, sultanas, apples, lemon rind and juice, salt and half the vinegar to the pan. Tie the spices in a muslin bag and add to the pan.

Cook gently until soft and pulpy, pressing the bag of spices occasionally with a wooden spoon. Stir in the sugar and the remaining vinegar and continue simmering until thick. Remove the bag of spices before putting into warm jars and covering.

Damson Chutney

A sweet chutney that makes a good accompaniment for ham.

MAKES APPROX. 1 KG (2 LB)
1 kg (2 lb) damsons
1 large onion
175 g (6 oz) dates
1 x 2.5 ml spoon (½ teaspoon) ground allspice
1 x 2.5 ml spoon (½ teaspoon) ground ginger
600 ml (1 pint) vinegar
350 g (12 oz) sugar
1 x 5 ml spoon (1 teaspoon) salt

Wash the damsons and drain. Peel and chop the onion. Stone and chop the dates. Place the damsons, onion, dates and spices in a pan with the vinegar. Bring to the boil and simmer gently until the damsons are well broken down. Remove the stones as they rise to the surface. Add the sugar and salt and stir until dissolved then continue cooking gently until thick, stirring occasionally. Put into warm jars and cover.

Banana & Date Chutney

MAKES APPROX. 1 KG (2 LB)
6 bananas
250 g (8 oz) dates
500 g (1 lb) onions
300 ml (½ pint) vinegar
250 g (8 oz) golden syrup
125 g (4 oz) crystallized ginger,
or 2 x 5 ml spoons (2 teaspoons) ground ginger
1 x 5 ml spoon (1 teaspoon) curry powder

Peel and slice the bananas. Stone and chop the dates. Peel and slice the onions. Place the dates, onions and bananas in a saucepan with the vinegar. Bring to the boil and simmer until tender. Add the, syrup and spices (first chop the crystallized ginger, if using) and cook gently, stirring occasionally, until thick. Pot into warm jars and cover. Ready for use in 3 weeks.

Blackberry Chutney

Blackberry chutney is a delicious accompaniment for fish or duck.

MAKES APPROX. 2–2.25 KG (4–4½ LB)
1.5 kg (3 lb) blackberries
750 g (1½ lb) cooking apples
350 g (12 oz) onions
600 ml (1 pint) white vinegar
2 x 5 ml spoons (2 teaspoons) ground ginger
1 x 5 ml spoon (1 teaspoon) ground mace
1 x 5 ml spoon (1 teaspoon) dry mustard
500 g (1 lb) sugar
1 x 15 ml spoon (1 tablespoon) salt

Pick over the blackberries, wash well and drain. Peel, core and chop the apples. Peel and chop the onions. Place the blackberries, apples and onions in a pan with the vinegar and spices. Bring to the boil, then simmer gently until tender (the pieces of onion should be really soft), stirring occasionally.

If you want the chutney to be seedless, sieve at this stage and return the sieved mixture to a clean pan. Add the sugar and salt, and stir until dissolved. Return to the boil and cook gently until thick, stirring occasionally. Pot into warm jars and cover.

Red Tomato Chutney

Distilled spiced vinegar gives the best colour for this chutney, but, as an alternative, use ordinary malt vinegar and add a pinch of ground mixed spice. Try it with kedgeree – it may sound unusual, but it is delicious!

MAKES APPROX. 2 KG (4 LB)
3 kg (6 lb) ripe tomatoes
500 g (1 lb) onions
25 g (1 oz) salt
2 x 5 ml spoons (2 teaspoons) paprika
pinch cayenne
300 ml (½ pint) distilled spiced vinegar
400 g (12 oz) sugar

Peel and chop the tomatoes. Peel and mince the onions. Put the tomatoes and onions in a pan and cook until soft and pulpy. Add the salt, spices and half the vinegar and simmer for 40 minutes. Stir in the sugar and remainder of the vinegar. Continue cooking until thick, then pot into warm jars and cover.

Tomato Chutney

To keep the bright colour of tomatoes in chutney, do not add sugar until the last 30 minutes of cooking time.

Gooseberry Chutney

This is an ideal chutney to serve with oily fish, particularly mackerel.

MAKES APPROX. 2 KG (4 LB)

1. 5 kg (3 lb) gooseberries
250 g (8 oz) onions
water
350 g (12 oz) seedless raisins, sultanas or dates
1 x 15 ml spoon (1 tablespoon) salt
1 x 15 ml spoon (1 tablespoon) ground ginger
1 x 5 ml spoon (1 teaspoon) ground mixed spice
600 ml (1 pint) vinegar
250 g (8 oz) sugar

Wash, and top and tail the gooseberries. Peel and chop the onions. Put the gooseberries and onions in a pan with a little water and cook gently until soft and pulpy. If using dates, stone and chop them. Add the raisins, sultanas or dates, salt, spices and half the vinegar to the pan. Continue cooking until the mixture thickens. Stir in the sugar and remaining vinegar and simmer gently until thick again. Pot into warm jars and cover.

Cranberry or Redcurrant Chutney

MAKES APPROX. 1 KG (2 LB)
500 g (1 lb) cranberries or redcurrants
500 g (1 lb) cooking apples
175 g (6 oz) seedless raisins
300 ml (½ pint) vinegar
pinch salt
2 x 5 ml spoons (2 teaspoons) whole mixed pickling spices
250 g (8 oz) sugar

Wash the cranberries or redcurrants. Peel, core and chop the apples. Put the cranberries and apples in a saucepan with the raisins, half the vinegar, the salt, and the spices tied in a muslin bag. Bring to the boil, stirring occasionally, and simmer until the fruit is soft. Add the remaining vinegar and the sugar and stir until it has dissolved. Cook gently until thick. Remove the bag of spices. Pot into warm jars and cover. Ready for use in 3 weeks.

Potting Chutney

When potting chutney, particularly if intended for show or competition, use a flat piece of clean wood to push the chutney down into the corners of the jar, and to remove any air bubbles.

Relishes

RELISHES are generally made from the same kinds of fruits and vegetables as chutneys, but the finished texture is different. The fruit or vegetables are coarsely chopped, spices and seasoning are added and vinegar is used as the preservative. Very easy to make, not all relishes require cooking, and, as with chutneys, there is plenty of scope for individual ideas in flavourings and combinations of ingredients.

Good with cold meats, salads and cheeses, relishes can also be used as a flavouring in casseroles and curries, or as an accompaniment to a hot curry.

Equipment

As for chutneys (see page 64).

Four Seasons Relish

MAKES APPROX. 1 KG (2 LB)
500 g (1 lb) dried apricots
water
2 shallots
2 dried chillies
125 g (4 oz) preserved or crystallized ginger
500 g (1 lb) brown sugar
1 x 5 ml spoon (1 teaspoon) salt
300 ml (½ pint) white wine vinegar
1 orange
25 g (1 oz) almonds

Wash the apricots, cover with cold water and leave to soak for 12–24 hours. Next day, simmer the fruit in the soaking water until tender. Peel and finely chop the shallots. De-seed the chillies and cut the chillies and ginger into slivers. Put the shallots, chillies and ginger in a pan with the sugar, salt and the vinegar. Grate the orange rind and squeeze the juice. Add both to the pan and boil, stirring to dissolve the sugar. Add the drained apricots, cut into quarters, and simmer for 20–25 minutes, stirring occasionally.

Blanch and chop the almonds and add for the last 10 minutes of cooking. Pot into warm jars and cover. Keep the relish for 6–8 weeks before using it.

Date Relish

MAKES APPROX. 1 KG (2 LB)
750 ml (1¼ pints) vinegar
50 g (2 oz) whole mixed pickling spices
pinch salt
1 kg (2 lb) stoned dates

Boil the vinegar, spices and salt together for 10 minutes. Pack the dates into warm jars and pour over the hot strained vinegar. Cover and keep for 8–10 weeks before using.

Tomato Relish

MAKES APPROX. 2 KG (4 LB)
2 kg (4 lb) ripe tomatoes
750 g (1½ lb) onions
25 g (1 oz) salt
3 large celery stalks
1 red pepper or another celery stalk
500 g (1 lb) granulated sugar
1 x 15 ml spoon (1 tablespoon) mustard seeds
450 ml (¾ pint) vinegar, preferably white

Peel and finely chop the tomatoes and onions. Mix together in a bowl, sprinkle with the salt and leave overnight if possible.

Next morning, rinse the tomatoes and onions under cold running water and drain well. Clean and finely chop the celery. De-seed and finely chop the pepper, if used. Mix the celery and pepper together in a large bowl with the sugar, mustard seeds and vinegar. Stir in the tomatoes and onions. Pot into warm jars and cover. Keep for at least 6 weeks before using.

Sweet Corn Relish

This is not as sweet as the Corn & Pepper Relish opposite.

MAKES APPROX. 1.5 KG (3 LB)
5 corn cobs
½ small white cabbage
2 small or 1 large onion
600 ml (1 pint) white vinegar
125 g (4 oz) sugar
2 x 5 ml spoons (2 teaspoons) salt
1 x 15 ml spoon (1 tablespoon) dry mustard
1 x 5 ml spoon (1 teaspoon) turmeric

Remove the husks and silk from the corn. Boil for 3 minutes, then strip the kernels from the cobs. Core and shred the cabbage. Peel and chop the onions. Put the vinegar, sugar, salt and spices in a pan and stir to dissolve the sugar. Bring to the boil and add the corn, cabbage and onion. Simmer gently until the vegetables are tender, stirring occasionally. Pot into warm jars and cover. Keep for at least 6 weeks before using.

Cucumber Relish

This is a good way of using misshapen cucumbers.

MAKES APPROX. 2 KG (4 LB)
3 large cucumbers
4 medium onions
50 g (2 oz) cooking salt
600 ml (1 pint) white vinegar
175 g (6 oz) sugar
1 x 5 ml spoon (1 teaspoon) celery seeds
1 x 5 ml spoon (1 teaspoon) mustard seeds

Wipe the cucumbers, but do not peel. Cut into small cubes. Peel and chop the onions. Layer the cucumber and onions in a bowl with the salt and leave for 1–2 hours. Tip into a colander and drain well. Put the vinegar, sugar and spices in a pan and stir to dissolve the sugar. Bring to the boil and simmer gently for 3–4 minutes.

Pack the drained vegetables into warm jars and cover immediately with the hot vinegar mixture (including the spices). This relish can be used after 4 weeks.

Corn & Pepper Relish

MAKES APPROX. 1.75 KG (3½ LB)
6 corn cobs
2 large onions
2 red peppers
2 green peppers
2 x 5 ml spoons (2 teaspoons) salt
2 x 5 ml spoons (2 teaspoons) flour
1 x 5 ml spoon (1 teaspoon) turmeric
2 x 5 ml spoons (2 teaspoons) dry mustard
250 g (8 oz) white sugar
600 ml (1 pint) white vinegar

Remove the husks and silk from the ears of corn, then boil for 3–5 minutes. Cool and strip off the corn kernels. Peel and chop the onions. Core, seed and chop the peppers.

Mix together the salt, flour, turmeric, mustard and sugar in a saucepan and stir in the vinegar. Add the corn, onions and peppers. Stir well. Bring to the boil and simmer for 30 minutes, stirring occasionally. Pot into warm jars and cover. Ready for use in 3 weeks.

Gooseberry Relish

This relish will keep for 3–4 months but check the level of vinegar occasionally and top up if necessary.

MAKES APPROX. 750 G (1½ LB)
500 g (1 lb) gooseberries
125–175 g (4–6 oz) shallots
250 g (8 oz) sultanas or seedless raisins
125 g (4 oz) sugar
1 x 15 ml spoon (1 tablespoon) dry mustard
1 x 5 ml spoon (1 teaspoon) ground ginger
300 ml (½ pint) vinegar

Wash, top and tail and chop the gooseberries. Peel and chop the shallots. Chop the sultanas or raisins. Place the gooseberries, shallots and sultanas or raisins in a large bowl. Add the sugar, mustard and ginger and mix thoroughly. Allow to stand for 1 hour, then mix again and pack into warm jars. Pour over the cold vinegar and cover. Ready for use in 2 weeks.

Apple & Pepper Relish

Another hot one!

MAKES APPROX. 1 KG (2 LB)
1 small cucumber
2 large onions
2 cooking apples
12 dried chillies
1 x 15 ml spoon (1 tablespoon) salt
250 g (8 oz) sugar
300 ml (½ pint) white vinegar

Peel the cucumber and onions and finely chop or mince coarsely. Peel, core and finely chop the apples. Put all these ingredients in a bowl. Crush or finely chop the chillies and add to the bowl. Mix together the salt, sugar and vinegar and stir until the sugar has dissolved (caster sugar dissolves faster). Pack the vegetable mixture into warm jars and fill with the vinegar. Cover. Keep for 3 weeks before using.

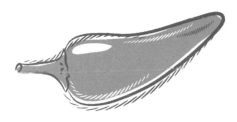

Mustard Relish

MAKES APPROX. 2 KG (4 LB)
1.5 kg/3 lb) cooking apples
500 g (1 lb) onions
1 litre (2 pints) vinegar
1 x 15 ml spoon (1 tablespoon) mustard seeds
2 x 5 ml spoons (2 teaspoons) dry mustard
250 g (8 oz) sultanas or seedless raisins
500 g (1 lb) sugar
1 x 15 ml spoon (1 tablespoon) salt

Peel, core and chop the apples. Peel and finely chop the onions. Put the apples, onions and half the vinegar in a pan. Add the mustard seeds in a muslin bag. Cook until tender. Mix the dry mustard with the rest of the vinegar and add with the remaining ingredients to the pan. Stir to dissolve the sugar, then cook gently until thick. Remove the mustard seeds before potting into warm jars and covering. Keep for at least 6 weeks before using.

Bengal Relish

Use this sparingly because it is very hot!

MAKES APPROX. 3 KG (6 LB)
2 kg (4 lb) green tomatoes
1 small white cabbage
750 g (1½ lb) onions
1 green pepper
1 red pepper
small piece horseradish
125 g (4 oz) salt
vinegar
500 g (1 lb) sugar
1 x 5 ml spoon (1 teaspoon) cinnamon
1 x 5 ml spoon (1 teaspoon) nutmeg
1 x 5 ml spoon (1 teaspoon) allspice
1 x 5 ml spoon (1 teaspoon) celery seed
1 x 5 ml spoon (1 teaspoon) mustard seed

Wash and chop the tomatoes. Wash, core and shred the cabbage. Peel and chop the onions, and de-seed and chop the peppers. Put all these ingredients in large bowl, peel and grate in the horseradish, sprinkle with the salt and allow to stand overnight.

Next morning, stir the vegetables, then tip into colander and run cold water through them. Drain well. Put in a saucepan and cover with cold water. Bring to the boil and drain. Almost cover with vinegar, add the sugar and spices and bring to boiling point. Simmer for 7 minutes, stirring occasionally. Pot into warm jars and cover. Keep for 4–6 weeks before use.

Cabbage & Beetroot Relish

Vary the amount of horseradish, depending on whether you like a strong, hot taste or one that is a little milder. Try to use the hard, white variety of cabbage for this recipe.

MAKES APPROX. 2 KG (4 LB)
1 kg (2 lb) beetroot
1 kg (2 lb) cabbage
25–50 g (1–2 oz) horseradish
275 g (9 oz) sugar, preferably white
600 ml (1 pint) vinegar
1 x 5 ml spoon (1 teaspoon) salt
1 x 15 ml spoon (1 tablespoon) dry mustard
pinch pepper

Wash the beetroot and cook until tender. Peel and chop finely. Core and shred the cabbage, then wash and drain well. Peel and grate the horseradish and put in a pan with the beetroot, cabbage and the rest of the ingredients. Mix well. Bring to the boil and cook for 20–30 minutes, depending on the crispness preferred. Pot into warm jars and cover. Ready for use after 2 weeks.

Relishes for Competitions

Do not put relishes into show or exhibition as chutney or pickles. They should be judged in a separate class.

Beetroot Relish

MAKES APPROX. 1 KG (2 LB)
500 g (1 lb) cooked, peeled beetroot
500 g (1 lb) white cabbage
250 g (8 oz) sugar
2 x 15 ml spoons (2 tablespoons) grated or dried horseradish
1 x 15 ml spoon (1 tablespoon) dry mustard
1 x 5 ml spoon (1 teaspoon) salt
pinch black pepper
600 ml (1 pint) vinegar

Chop the beetroot roughly. Wash, core and shred the cabbage. Put these in a pan with all the other ingredients and stir to dissolve the sugar. Simmer gently for 30 minutes. Pot into warm jars and cover. Keep for at least 6 weeks before using.

Date & Apple Relish

MAKES APPROX. 2.25 KG (4½ LB)
500 g (1 lb) cooking apples
500 g (1 lb) onions
500 g (1 lb) black dates
500 g (1 lb) sultanas or seedless raisins
500 g (1 lb) sugar
600 ml (1 pint) white or malt vinegar
25 g (1 oz) whole mixed pickling spices

Peel, core and mince or finely chop the apples. Peel and mince or finely chop the onions. Stone the dates and mince or finely chop with the sultanas or raisins. Place the apples, onions, dates and sultanas or raisins in a bowl with the sugar and vinegar and stir well. Tie the spices in muslin and add to the bowl. Leave for 24–48 hours, stirring occasionally.

Remove the bag of spices. Pot into warm jars and cover. The relish will be ready for use in 2 weeks.

Apple Relish

MAKES APPROX. 1.5 KG (3 LB)
1. 5 kg (3 lb) cooking apples
75 g (3 oz) salt
10–12 shallots
900 ml (1½ pints) vinegar
375 g (12 oz) sugar
25 g (1 oz) turmeric
12 g (½ oz) ground ginger
12 whole cloves
12 whole peppercorns

Peel and core the apples. Cut into bite-size cubes and spread on a dish. Sprinkle with the salt and leave for 24 hours.

Peel and chop the shallots and put in a saucepan with the vinegar, sugar, turmeric and ginger. Tie the cloves and peppercorns in muslin and add to the pan. Bring to the boil, stirring occasionally, then boil hard for 10 minutes.

Rinse and drain the apples. Remove the bag of spices from the pan and add the apples. Cook gently for 10–15 minutes, or until tender, without allowing the apples to break up, if possible. Pot into warm jars and cover. Ready for use in 2–3 weeks.

Sauces

SAUCES are regarded as a stimulant to the digestion and as an appetizer. Like chutneys and relishes, they can be made from a variety of fruit and vegetables, with the addition of spices and vinegar. As a general rule, the ingredients for a sauce are either minced or chopped, then cooked, sieved and re-cooked to a creamy, pouring consistency, somewhere between single and double cream. If, after cooking and bottling, the fruit tissues separate out in the bottle, leaving a clear fluid at the top, further cooking will usually remedy this. As with chutneys, sauces should be cooked in an uncovered pan.

Those sauces made from ingredients low in acid content, for example mushrooms and ripe tomatoes, have to be sterilized after bottling, but this is a fairly simple process.

Equipment

As for chutneys and relishes (see page 64), with the addition of suitable bottles for storing sauces. A heatproof jug facilitates the filling of bottles.

Sterilizing Procedure

If using corks, tie them down to prevent them blowing out during sterilizing. Tighten screw caps, give a half turn back to loosen slightly. Make a false bottom of slatted wood, straw or folded newspaper in a deep pan. Stand the bottles in the pan, making sure they do not touch each other or the sides of the pan, and add enough warm water to come up to the bottom of the corks or screw tops. Bring the water up to 77°C, 170°F and keep at this temperature for 30 minutes. If you have not got a sugar thermometer to check the temperature, heat the water slowly until tiny bubbles are rising up from the bottom of the pan. Maintain at this stage for 30 minutes, taking, in all, about 1½ hours to complete the process. After this, remove the bottles from the pan, tighten the screw tops or push in the corks. When they are completely cold and dry, dip the corks into melted paraffin wax to make an airtight seal.

General Points

• If using corks, they must be new and should be boiled for 10 minutes or kept submerged in boiling water for 15 minutes before use. This not only sterilizes them and prevents them going mouldy during storage, but also softens them, making them easier to insert. Screw tops should be similarly sterilized.

• A fine film of paraffin wax should be run over the cork and top of the bottle to provide an airtight seal. Alternatively, squares of plastic may be placed over the cork and tied tightly around the neck of the bottle to exclude all air.

Ripe Tomato Sauce

Use white vinegar if possible, as this helps to keep a true
tomato colour. To make a more economical sauce, substitute apples
for half the tomatoes, but obviously this will not give such
a good tomato colour and flavour.

MAKES APPROX. 1.5 LITRES (3 PINTS)
3 kg (6 lb) tomatoes
1 x 5 ml spoon (1 teaspoon) ground ginger
1 x 5 ml spoon (1 teaspoon) ground allspice
1 x 5 ml spoon (1 teaspoon) ground mace
1 x 5 ml spoon (1 teaspoon) ground cloves
1 x 15 ml spoon (1 tablespoon) salt
300 ml (½ pint) vinegar, preferably white
250 g (8 oz) sugar

Wash the tomatoes and cook until tender. Dissolve the spices and salt
in the vinegar in another pan. Rub the tomato pulp through a sieve and
add to the spiced vinegar. Bring to the boil and simmer gently until the
consistency of cream. Add the sugar and stir until dissolved, maintaining
the creamy consistency. Pour into warm bottles and seal. This sauce will
require sterilizing (see page 99), or it will keep for only 2–3 weeks.

Red Tomato Sauce

Being lightly spiced, this sauce has a good tomato colour
and flavour.

MAKES APPROX. 1 LITRE (2 PINTS)
3 kg (6 lb) ripe red tomatoes
3 celery stalks or 1 x 5 ml spoon (1 teaspoon) celery salt
1 x 15 ml spoon (1 tablespoon) salt
250 g (8 oz) sugar
2 x 5 ml spoons (2 teaspoons) paprika
pinch cayenne pepper
300 ml (½ pint) vinegar

Wash the tomatoes and celery, if used, and chop them. Put in a pan and
cook slowly until pulped, stirring occasionally. Press through a sieve
and return the purée to a clean pan. Add the remaining ingredients and
stir until the sugar has dissolved. Bring to the boil and simmer gently
until the sauce has thickened. Pour into warm bottles and seal. This
sauce will not keep longer than 4 weeks unless sterilized (see page 99)
or frozen.

Sauces for Competitions

Sauces entered for show or competition should be in suitable
containers, such as sauce bottles of clear glass with no proprietary
brand marks. Seal with either a screw top or cork, and leave
roughly 1–2.5-cm (½–1-in) headspace between the sauce and top
of the bottle or cork.

Rhubarb Sauce

MAKES APPROX. 1 LITRE (2 PINTS)
1.25 kg (2½ lb) rhubarb
1.25 kg (2½ lb) onions
1 x 5 ml spoon (1 teaspoon) crushed chillies
1 x 5 ml spoon (1 teaspoon) peppercorns
1 x 5 ml spoon (1 teaspoon) curry powder
1 x 5 ml spoon (1 teaspoon) ground ginger
2 x 5 ml spoons (2 teaspoons) salt
1 litre (2 pints) malt vinegar
750 g (1½ lb) brown sugar

Wipe the rhubarb and cut into chunks. Peel and slice the onions. Put the rhubarb and onions in a pan and add the chillies, spices, salt and half the vinegar. Simmer for 1–1½ hours, stirring occasionally.

Press the pulp through a sieve and return to a clean pan. Add the sugar and stir until dissolved. If the mixture seems thin, add only 300 ml (½ pint) of the remaining vinegar. Simmer until the sauce is creamy in consistency. Pour the sauce into warm bottles and seal.

Cranberry Sauce

MAKES APPROX. 600 ML (1 PINT)
500 g (1lb) cranberries
150 ml (¼ pint) vinegar
1 x 5 ml spoon (1 teaspoon) ground allspice
1 x 2.5 ml spoon (½ teaspoon) ground cloves
1 x 2.5 ml spoon (½ teaspoon) ground cinnamon
500 g (1 lb) sugar, preferably a mixture of
brown and white

Wash the cranberries and put in a pan with the vinegar and spices. Cook gently until the fruit is soft and mushy. Add the sugar and stir until it has dissolved. Bring to the boil and boil hard for 5 minutes. Sieve, then put in a clean pan. Return to the boil and boil for a further 1 minute. Pour into warm bottles and seal.

Plum Sauce

MAKES APPROX. 1 LITRE (2 PINTS)
2 kg (4 lb) plums
250 g (8 oz) onions
125 g (4 oz) currants
4 chillies
2 pieces dried root ginger
1 x 5 ml spoon (1 teaspoon) peppercorns
1 x 5 ml spoon (1 teaspoon) whole allspice
600 ml (1 pint) vinegar
250 g (8 oz) sugar
25 g (1 oz) salt

Wash the plums, cut into halves or quarters and remove the stones. Peel and chop the onions. Put the plums and onions in a pan, and add the currants, chillies, spices and half the vinegar. Bring to the boil and simmer for 30 minutes, stirring occasionally. Rub the pulp through a sieve and return to a clean pan. Stir in the sugar, salt and remaining vinegar. Simmer for a further 1 hour, stirring occasionally. Pour into warm bottles and seal.

Apple Sauce

MAKES APPROX. 600 ML (1 PINT)
1.25 kg (2½ lb) cooking apples
1 large onion
6 cloves
1 x 5 ml spoon (1 teaspoon) ground ginger
pinch cayenne pepper
300 ml (½ pint) vinegar
125 g (4 oz) brown sugar
1 x 5 ml spoon (1 teaspoon) salt

Peel, core and chop the apples. Peel and slice the onion. Put the apples, onion, spices and half the vinegar in a pan. Cook until pulpy, stirring occasionally. Press the pulp through a sieve and return to a clean pan. Add the sugar, salt and remaining vinegar, stirring, until the sugar is dissolved. Simmer gently for 10–15 minutes. Pour into warm bottles and seal. Use within 4 weeks (unless the sauce is sterilized, see page 99).

Mushroom Ketchup

Use the larger flat mushrooms for this sauce and preferably
when they are 24–48 hours old. It is a very thin liquid.

MAKES APPROX. 900 ML (1½ PINTS)
750 g (1½ lb) mushrooms
50 g (2 oz) salt
300 ml (½ pint) vinegar
1 x 5 ml spoon (1 teaspoon) peppercorns
1 x 2.5 ml spoon (½ teaspoon) ground allspice
large pinch each of ground mace, ginger, cloves and cinnamon

Wipe the mushrooms, if necessary, and peel them. Break into small pieces, place in a bowl and sprinkle with the salt. Leave for about 12 hours, then rinse and drain. Mash well with a wooden spoon, place in a pan and add the vinegar and spices. Bring to the boil, then cover and simmer for 30 minutes. Strain through a sieve. Pour into warm bottles and seal.

This ketchup must be sterilized immediately. Place the bottles in a pan of hot water with a false bottom. Bring the water to simmering point, and simmer for 30 minutes (see page 99).

Green Tomato Sauce

If you like, you can add a few drops of gravy browning to this sauce to improve the colour.

MAKES APPROX. 900 ML (1½ PINTS)
1. 5 kg (3 lb) green tomatoes
500 g (1 lb) cooking apples
125 g (4 oz) shallots or onions
250 g (8 oz) sugar, preferably brown
300 ml (½ pint) vinegar
1 x 15 ml spoon (1 tablespoon) salt
1 x 5 ml spoon (1 teaspoon) ground mixed spice
1 x 2.5 ml spoon (½ teaspoon) black or cayenne pepper
1 x 2.5 ml spoon (½ teaspoon) dry mustard

Wash the tomatoes and apples, and peel the shallots or onions. Chop them all thickly and put in a pan with all the other ingredients. Bring to the boil, stirring occasionally, and simmer for 1–1½ hours, until the vegetables and fruit are really soft. Sieve the sauce and return to a clean pan. Return to the boil and boil for 1 minute. Pour into warm bottles and seal.

Pear Sauce or Ketchup

MAKES APPROX. 600 ML (1 PINT)
1 kg (2 lb) pears
water
175 g (6 oz) sugar
150 ml (¼ pint) vinegar
1 x 5 ml spoon (1 teaspoon) salt
1 x 2.5 ml spoon (½ teaspoon) ground cloves
1 x 2.5 ml spoon (½ teaspoon) ground cinnamon
1 x 2.5 ml spoon (½ teaspoon) pepper

Wash and stalk the pears, then chop roughly. Put in a pan with a very little water and cook until soft. Press through a sieve. Tip the pear purée into a clean pan and add all the other ingredients. Bring to the boil, stirring occasionally, and simmer gently until the sauce has thickened. Pour into warm bottles and seal.

Mint Sauce

This sauce should keep at least 6 months.
When you want to use it, dilute it to taste with
more vinegar or lemon juice.

MAKES APPROX. 300 ML (½ PINT)
300 ml (½ pint) vinegar
175 g (6 oz) sugar
75 g (3 oz) mint

Heat the vinegar and sugar together, stirring to dissolve the sugar. Bring to the boil and boil for 1 minute. Remove from the heat. Wash the mint, drain well and chop. Add to the saucepan of vinegar, stir well and cook for 1–2 minutes. Allow to cool completely before potting into warm bottles.

Gooseberry Sauce

This sauce is light brown. If you want a green colour, use young gooseberries, white vinegar and root ginger tied in muslin.

MAKES APPROX. 900 ML (1½ PINTS)
1. 5 kg (3 lb) gooseberries
350 g (12 oz) onions
600 ml (1 pint) vinegar
1 x 15 ml spoon (1 tablespoon) ground ginger
1 x 5 ml spoon (1 teaspoon) cayenne pepper
1 x2.5 ml spoon (½ teaspoon) salt
500 g (1 lb) sugar

Wash the gooseberries. Peel and slice the onions. Put the gooseberries and onions in a pan with the spices, salt and half the vinegar. Cook until soft. Press the pulp through a sieve and return to a clean pan. Stir in the sugar and the remainder of the vinegar and cook gently until creamy. Pour into warm bottles and seal.

Haw Sauce

MAKES APPROX. 600 ML (1 PINT)
750 g (1½ lb) haws
450 ml (¾ pint) vinegar
125 g (4 oz) sugar
25 g (1 oz) salt
1 x 2.5 ml spoon (½ teaspoon) ground pepper

Wash the haws and put in a pan with the vinegar. Cook gently for 30–40 minutes. Press through a sieve, then put in a clean pan with the sugar, salt and pepper. Bring to the boil, stirring occasionally, and simmer for 10 minutes. Pour into warm bottles and seal.

Vinegars

VINEGARS, flavoured with fruit, vegetables or herbs, were used far more in cooking 100 years ago than today, but over the past few years or so interest in flavoured vinegars has revived. As they are very easy to make and inexpensive, a variety of flavoured vinegars in the kitchen cupboard can give added interest to such things as salad dressings, sauces, cold meats, drinks and grilled meat and fish.

Equipment

Bowls Large earthenware or glass.
Wooden spoons.
Scales.
Knives.
Bottles With screw tops or corks. As with sauces (see page 99), corks and screw tops should be boiled for 10 minutes before use.

General Points

• Pick herbs just before they come into flower, and preferably in the early morning, before the sun gets too strong. Use good-quality vegetables and fruit in order to obtain the best flavour.

• Keep fruit vinegars in a dark cupboard to prevent loss of colour.

• Wine vinegar, though a little more expensive, is the best for most recipes, as it is less harsh than malt vinegar, and will not mask the flavours imparted by the fruit, herbs or vegetables. If malt vinegar is suitable, this will be stated in the recipe.

- When steeping herb vinegars to extract the maximum flavour, it is essential that the container is tightly covered. Acetic add is volatile and, if the bowl or jar is covered merely with a cloth, it will be lost. A large jar, with a screw-top lid, is the best thing to use.

- In nearly all of these recipes, the amount made will depend entirely on how much vinegar you use.

Celery Vinegar

1 large head celery
wine vinegar

Wash the celery thoroughly and remove any decayed parts. Chop the stalks and leaves finely and place in a large jar or bowl. Cover with wine vinegar and leave, covered tightly, for 2 weeks, stirring occasionally. Strain and bottle.

Tarragon Vinegar

Apart from its uses in cooking, tarragon vinegar is supposed to cure, or at least to alleviate, bee stings.

sprays of tarragon
white wine vinegar

Half fill a 600-ml (1-pint) jar or bowl with fresh tarragon leaves, previously washed and drained. Cover with wine vinegar and leave, covered, for 4 weeks, stirring occasionally. Strain and bottle, adding a fresh spray of tarragon to each bottle before corking.

Other herbs, such as thyme, marjoram, dill or sage can be used for this recipe. Sage vinegar is supposed to be an aid to digestion: for this, dilute 1 x 15 ml spoon (1 tablespoon) in an equal amount of hot water.

Cucumber Vinegar

MAKES APPROX. 1 LITRE (2 PINTS)
4 large cucumbers
3 medium onions
1 litre (2 pints) wine vinegar

Peel and finely chop the cucumbers and onions. Place in a large bowl or jar and cover with the vinegar. Leave, covered tightly, for a week, stirring occasionally. Strain and bottle.

Chilli Vinegar

MAKES APPROX. 1 LITRE (2 PINTS)
50–75 g (2–3 oz) red chillies
1 litre (2 pints) malt vinegar

Split the chillies in half and place in a jar or bowl. Cover with the vinegar. Leave, covered, for 4 weeks, stirring occasionally. Strain and bottle.

Onion Vinegar

MAKES APPROX. 1 LITRE (2 PINTS)
125 g (4 oz) onions
1 litre (2 pints) white wine vinegar

Peel and finely chop the onions and put in a jar or bowl. Pour over the vinegar and leave, covered, for 2 weeks, stirring occasionally. Strain and bottle.

Garlic can be used instead of onion, if preferred, but you would, of course, need far less.

Fruit Vinegars

Generally made from fruits such as blackberries, raspberries and blackcurrants, these vinegars are used as a flavouring for puddings, or diluted with water or soda water to make a refreshing drink. They make a soothing balm for sore throats, too.

Raspberry Vinegar

1 kg (2 lb) raspberries
1 litre (2 pints) wine vinegar

Pick over the fruit, making sure none is decayed or over-ripe, and place in a bowl or jar. Bruise the fruit gently with a wooden spoon and cover with the vinegar. Cover the bowl and leave for 4 days, stirring occasionally. Strain the juice through clean muslin or cotton into a saucepan. Bring to the boil and boil for 10 minutes. Bottle while hot and seal.

For a sweet vinegar, dissolve 350 g (12 oz) sugar in each 600 ml (1 pint) of the strained liquid just before boiling.

Vinegars for Competitions

It is unusual to find a class for flavoured vinegars in a show but, if there is, the same rules apply: clear glass bottles with no proprietary brand names, and the contents and date stated on the label.

Flower Vinegars

Mention is made of these vinegars in many old cookery or household books and they seem to have been used mainly as a toilet preparation, or to be sprinkled in a sick room. The following recipe may be of interest to anyone with a flower garden.

25 g (1 oz) approx. scented pink petals
25 g (1 oz) approx. scented red rose petals
25 g (1 oz) approx. rosemary petals
600 ml (1 pint) wine vinegar

Place the petals in a large heatproof bowl or jar. Bring the vinegar to the boil and pour over the petals. Cover tightly and leave for 10 days in a warm kitchen or airing cupboard, or somewhere with similar temperature. Stir once or twice a day. Strain the liquid through clean muslin or cotton and bottle.

Freezing &
Bottling

Freezing

FREEZING food at home, as a method of preservation, is a simple, quick and practically foolproof way of keeping produce from garden or orchard at its best for long periods. Before the advent of freezers and refrigerators, many large country houses had a cold room in the grounds of the house. These were underground rooms, lined with blocks of ice, where game, meat, fish and fruit were kept for quite long periods.

As with other methods of preservation, the home freezer, properly used, can provide a variety of food throughout the year, particularly at times when the supply of fresh fruit and vegetables is limited.

When buying a freezer, shop around and compare sizes, prices and models. Your choice will be governed by the space available in your house, and the size of your family.

There are advantages and disadvantages to both upright and chest freezers, but all freezers should be sited in a dry, cool and well-ventilated place. A freezer actually warms the surrounding air, hence the need for good ventilation. The weight of the freezer when fully loaded is considerable and this factor should also be taken into consideration, especially in an old house. Chest freezers have a wider base, thus distributing the weight.

Equipment

Fine wire mesh basket With handle, for blanching vegetables.
Saucepan With lid, capable of holding the wire basket.
Bowls Deep, for cooling vegetables.
Knives Stainless steel.
Sieves Stainless steel or nylon, or liquidizer.
Measuring jug Heatproof.
Metal trays For open freezing.
Labelling materials.
Cartons and packaging materials.
Chinagraph pencil.

General Points

• Try to make maximum use of your freezer space by being selective about the vegetables and fruit you freeze. Try to maintain a good variety and, of course, choose those foods that all the family like.

• Do not freeze more of one type of fruit or vegetable than you will need from one harvest to the next.

• All foods have a period of satisfactory storage. After that, they will begin to lose their quality and flavour. Freezer temperatures do not *stop* the chemical changes which spoil food; they only slow down their action.

• All foods must be frozen as quickly as possible. Slow freezing causes big ice crystals to form which rupture the cells and cause the moisture and juices to run out as the food thaws.

- Most freezers can only freeze up to one-tenth of their capacity in every 24 hours, so always check the manufacturer's handbook before planning a major freezing session.

- Freeze when food is in perfect condition and as soon as possible after gathering and preparing for the freezer. Handle and prepare small quantities at a time.

- Blanch vegetables before freezing and cool hot foods as rapidly as possible prior to freezing.

- Always use guaranteed moisture-proof and vapour-proof containers and packaging materials.

- Pack in sizes suitable for family and life style: 125 g (4 oz) of vegetables is an average portion per person per meal.

- Label and date packets and keep a log book or record of contents in and out.

- Always follow the manufacturer's instructions for your particular freezer when setting the temperature gauge for freezing fresh food. This is very important.

- To help you see at a glance what you have in your freezer, adopt some general system of storage, such as using one colour label for fresh vegetables, another for cooked foods, etc. Alternatively, keep foods of similar type in baskets or string or polythene bags.

- Never leave the freezer open for longer than necessary.

- If growing your own fruit and vegetables, it is sensible to buy or plant the varieties that are known to freeze well.

- Air will cause frozen food to deteriorate, so exclude as much air as possible when packing food for freezing.

- Polythene bags are extremely useful for loose items, such as beans or sprouts. To make better use of your freezer space, put the bag in a square or oblong rigid carton, fill it with the fruit or vegetables and then freeze it all together. You will then have a frozen rectangular block (which you can remove from the carton) and which will be easier to stack in the freezer than an irregular shape.

• Rigid containers, whether made of plastic or waxed cardboard, are very useful in a freezer, as their regular shapes help to make the best use of freezer space.

• Plastic containers are the most expensive but they can be used repeatedly. They are particularly good for foods that can be packed into them without leaving any pockets of air. Wash thoroughly between use and be particularly careful if strong-flavoured foods, such as onions, curry or orange juice, have been stored in them.

• Waxed cartons are cheaper and ideal for fruits, purées, soups, etc. However, they do have a shorter freezer life, as they can normally be used only two or three times. Lining the waxed carton with a polythene bag before packing will help to prolong its life, but remember it must still be cleaned thoroughly between use. Never pour hot foods into waxed containers, as the heat may melt the wax, thus making the container porous.

• Most brands of ovenproof glassware will withstand freezing, providing the contents have been cooled before being placed in the freezer. In general, however, glass containers are not really suitable, as they are liable to become brittle at low temperatures.

• Liquid and semi-liquid food will expand while it is freezing, so headspace must be allowed between the food and the seal. As a general rule 1–2.5 cm (½–1 in) is sufficient as headspace, although this does depend somewhat on the quantity and type of food being frozen.

Methods of Freezing Fruit

Open-freezing This is recommended for berry fruit such as raspberries, strawberries, loganberries and blackberries. In fact, it is suitable for all types of fruit but it takes longer than other methods and is not so important for the harder type of fruits.

To open-freeze, hull the fruit as necessary, rinse in cold water if absolutely necessary and drain. If the fruit is clean enough to avoid rinsing, so much the better. Put the prepared fruit in single layers (not touching each other) on trays or dishes and freeze for 1–2 hours or until firm, then pack immediately into bags or containers. Seal and label.

Fruit that is open-frozen in this way can be eaten whole for desserts, as the shape is maintained. If you want the fruit as a filling for tarts and puddings, or to make into sauces or purées, it is not really worth the extra trouble to open-freeze. Instead, cook and cool the fruit, pack into polythene bags or containers, seal, label and freeze. This saves you both time and freezer space.

Sugar-freezing This is suitable for soft berry fruit, and can also be used for currants, cherries, gooseberries and blueberries.

Roll the prepared fruit in dry sugar using about 175 g (6 oz) caster sugar to each 500 g (1 lb) fruit, and pack in rigid containers. Fruit frozen in this way can be used whole for desserts, or in pies, tarts, puddings, sauces and purées. For the latter dishes, however, you would again save time and space by freezing the fruit after you have cooked it.

Some people also use this method to freeze fruit intended for jam-making at a later date. If you do so, you must make a note of the amount of sugar used, so that you can deduct this from the amount in the jam recipe. The exact weight of sugar used in the freezing process is not always too easy to calculate, however, and it is probably best to freeze the fruit without sugar (in polythene bags) if you intend to use it for jam-making.

Syrup-freezing This method is very good for fruit such as apricots, pears, peaches etc. Prepare a syrup of average strength: i.e., using about 250 g (8 6z) sugar to every 600 ml (1 pint) water. Bring to the boil, stirring to dissolve the sugar, then strain if necessary and allow to cool. Keep the syrup covered while cooling.

The strength of the syrup used in this method can be altered to suit individual taste. For soft fruits, many people prefer a heavier syrup of about 500 g (1 lb) sugar to 600 ml (1 pint) water. Allow about 300 ml (½ pint) syrup to each 500 g (1 lb) fruit and make sure the fruit is completely covered by the syrup, or the top layer may discolour or lack flavour. (A piece of crumpled greaseproof paper or foil placed on top will keep the fruit under the syrup.)

Notes The cut surfaces of some fruit, such as apples and peaches, turn brown when exposed to the air. To help prevent this, lemon juice or ascorbic acid can be added to the syrup solution. The disadvantage of using lemon juice is that, in the quantity required, the fruit will absorb too much of the lemon flavour. Ascorbic acid crystals (obtainable at chemists, health-food shops and online), on the other hand, do not have any effect on the flavour. The crystals should be dissolved in a little cold water and added to the syrup. The correct ratio is 200–300 mg ascorbic acid crystals to 500 g (1 lb) fruit. If you are unable to buy the crystals, use crushed Vitamin C tablets instead. Tablets are generally sold in strengths of 50–100 mg, so calculate how many you need accordingly.

Purées This is a very good way of preserving any misshapen or slightly damaged fruit, particularly when you have a surplus or a glut. Any type of fruit may be frozen like this, either as a fresh or cooked purée.

Prepare the fruit according to type, peeling if necessary and cutting away any bruised areas. For fresh purées, liquidize the fruit or rub through a sieve. The mixture can be sweetened to taste before freezing, or later when required for use. For cooked purées, simmer the prepared fruit in a very little water, then liquidize or sieve and sweeten if necessary. Allow to cool before freezing.

Strawberries, raspberries, gooseberries, damsons and apples are very useful as a sweetened purée as, once thawed, they can be used in a multitude of puddings with the minimum of preparation.

Thawing of Fruit

Whatever method of freezing is used, all fruit should be thawed slowly in unopened packets. This is particularly essential for soft fruits and those which discolour easily. Fruit which is likely to discolour, such as pears, peaches and apples, should, if possible, be kept submerged in syrup while thawing.

Dessert fruit is best served slightly chilled, so thawing overnight in the refrigerator is a good method.

If the fruit has not been frozen in syrup, float the bag in a bowl of cold water (warm water results in a poor texture) or in front of a fan, for quicker thawing.

When using fruit for stewing or jam-making, the frozen block can be placed in a pan and heated gently. Always completely thaw fruit intended as a pie filling before using it, otherwise the pastry base may be soggy.

Remember, if you want to use the fruit for jam-making, that the pectin content of fruit is reduced during freezer storage. This is particularly critical with fruit already low in pectin, such as strawberries. To offset this when jam-making, allow an extra tenth in weight of fruit; i.e., an extra 250 g (8 oz) to every 2.5 kg (5 lb) fruit called for in the recipe. Follow the recipe for the other ingredients in the jam.

Freezing Fruit Syrups

If you have a surplus of a particular fruit, or a quantity of fruit that is too ripe for freezing, bottling or jam-making, a good way of preserving it is to freeze it as a syrup. This can then be used as the basis for sauces, hot or cold drinks, iced lollies, jellies, etc. The best fruit for this is raspberries, strawberries, loganberries, blackberries and blackcurrants.

To make the syrup, wash the fruit in cold water if necessary and pick over. Place the fruit in a pan. When using the method for blackcurrants, add 300 ml (½ pint) water to every 500 g (1 lb) fruit. For blackberries, use 300 ml (½ pint) water to every 3 kg (6 lb) berries. Other fruit needs no water.

Heat the fruit, stirring constantly, and bring quickly to the boil, crushing any whole fruit with a wooden spoon. Boil for 1 minute, then tip the fruit into a jelly bag and allow it to drip for several hours, or overnight. Alternatively, strain the fruit through a sieve with a piece of muslin laid across it. (It can be strained through a sieve without any muslin, in which case a little more of the fruit tissue will remain in the syrup. This does not affect the flavour in any way.)

The sweetness of the syrup is a matter for individual taste but, generally, 350 g (12 oz) sugar to every 600 ml (1 pint) juice is recommended. Measure the juice, add the sugar and stir until dissolved. Strain again through muslin, cheesecloth, or a piece of fine cotton material.

Freeze the syrup as iced lollies, or in suitable containers and quantities as required for future use. Remember to leave an adequate headspace as the syrup will expand as it freezes.

Fruit Freezing Chart

FRUIT AND PREPARATION	METHOD
Apples	
1. Peel, core and cut into thick slices. Blanch for 1–2 minutes (according to the thickness of the slices). Cool rapidly. Alternatively, drop into water containing ascorbic acid. Drain.	In dry sugar; without sugar or in a medium syrup.
2. As purée.	Cook, then add sugar if you want a sweetened purée. Cool.
Apricots	
1. Halve and stone	In syrup, containing either 1 x 15 ml spoon (1 tablespoon) lemon juice per litre (2 pints) or ascorbic acid.
2. As purée.	Slightly over-ripe but sound apricots can be used for this. Peel, stone, then sieve or liquidize and sweeten to taste.
Currants (black, red or white)	
1. Whole: prepare, rinse and drain thoroughly.	Dry in bags, with or without sugar
2. As purée.	Cook, sieve and sweeten to taste. Cool.
Cherries (red varieties are the best for freezing)	
Remove stones and rinse and drain if necessary.	In syrup or dry sugar
Damsons	
1. Skins toughen if kept in a dry state for any length of time in a freezer but they are suitable for jam-making for up to 3 months' storage.	In syrup.
2. As purée	Cook, sieve and sweeten to taste. Cool.
Gooseberries	
1. Whole: rinse, top and tail. Drain well.	Dry in bags or in a syrup.
2. As purée	Cook, sieve and sweeten to taste. Cool.

FRUIT AND PREPARATION	METHOD
Pears	
Not really recommended for freezing, but if you want to do so, choose pears with strong flavour for best results. Peel, core and quarter; poach in boiling syrup for 2 minutes. Drain and cool.	In syrup. (Syrup in which pears were poached may be used, but add ascorbic acid.) Strain and cool.
Plums and greengages	
Rinse if necessary and dry. May be frozen whole or halved and stoned.	Dry in bags (but skin is inclined to toughen after a time with this method), or in syrup, halved and stoned.

SOFT FRUIT

Blackberries, loganberries,raspberries	
1. Rinse and drain if necessary and handle very carefully.	Open-freeze on trays then pack in bags or boxes or freeze in dry sugar for dessert use. Freeze plain for jam-making.
2. As purée.	Sieve or liquidize (sieve again if you want to remove all the pips). Sweeten to taste.
Strawberries	
1. These tend to collapse when thawed and, if frozen in syrup, are best eaten while still slightly chilled. Rinse only if absolutely necessary and drain.	Open-freeze on trays then pack in bags or freeze in syrup. (If packed dry in bags and frozen, they can be used for cooking/jam-making purposes.)
2. As purée (the best way of retaining the flavour).	Sieve or blend, sweeten to taste.
Tomatoes	
1. Rinse and drain.	Whole in bags. (They are then useful as they collapse when thawed.)
2. Sliced.	Open-freeze on trays, then pack in bags. (Useful for garnish on quiches, etc.)
3. As purée.	Cook and sieve.

Methods of Freezing Vegetables

As with fruit, all vegetables intended for freezing should be young, tender and at their peak for the best results. Once picked, preparation and freezing should be carried out as quickly as possible, so always try to pick and prepare in small quantities, if this is practical.

Salad vegetables do not freeze satisfactorily, as their high water content means they do not retain their crisp texture after thawing.

Certain vegetables, such as peas and broad, runner and French beans, can be open-frozen on trays before packing. Although this takes more time, the advantage is that they will 'run' easily from the bag when required, instead of coming out as one solid block. Most vegetables require blanching before freezing. This helps to retain the colour, conserve any Vitamin C present, and prevent development of poor or bad flavours from the action of enzymes.

Most vegetables can be cooked while still frozen, with the following exceptions: corn on the cob (must be thawed completely), mushrooms and courgettes (partially thaw, then fry gently in a little oil or butter or grill), new potatoes (warm through in hot water after thawing). Chips can be fried from the frozen state but even small quantities placed in heated fat or oil cause spluttering and steaming, so care must be taken. It is better to thaw chips in the unopened package for about 2 hours at room temperature.

Blanching Vegetables

Blanching is a simple and straightforward process but there are some essential rules to follow.

All prepared vegetables should be blanched in not less than 3 litres (6 pints) boiling water to each 500 g (1 lb) vegetables, so that the water can circulate around the vegetables, and returned to boiling point in 1 minute after the vegetables have been added to the blanching pan.

If using a metal basket for blanching heat it in the blanching water before adding the vegetables.

Lightly salted water – 2 x 15 ml spoons (2 tablespoons) salt to each 3 litres (6 pints) water – helps to retain the colour of the vegetables.

Be sure to follow the blanching times as shown in the chart on pages 127–9. These are important for safe results.

After blanching, lift out the vegetables and plunge them into ice cold water. This rapid cooling is essential to prevent over-cooking, and vegetables should be cooled for the same amount of time as they were blanched. Ice cubes added to the water will help the cooling process.

After cooling, drain well before packing for the freezer. Some people recommend drying by tipping on to clean tea towels but there is a danger of subjecting the vegetables to germs and bacteria. Careful draining is better.

Note If freezing mixed vegetables for a macedoine or stew pack, blanch each vegetable separately, then mix them. Remember to label packs particularly carefully, so you know exactly what they contain.

Freezing Herbs

Fresh herbs can be frozen but become limp when thawed and so are unsuitable for garnishing. However, they are very useful in soups, stews, sauces, savoury butters, etc. The amount and type of herbs used in a household is obviously a matter of individual taste but, generally speaking, mint, parsley, chives and perhaps tarragon are most often required in cooking.

Herbs do not need blanching, although dipping momentarily in boiling water helps to keep the colour. They can be frozen whole in sprigs or chopped, but they will go brown after about 3 months in the freezer. Pick before they have started to flower, wash and pat dry. Pack the sprigs into bags. You can crumble these from the frozen state straight into soups, casseroles, etc. for flavouring.

Mint, parsley and chives can be finely chopped and then frozen with a little water in ice-cube trays. The frozen cubes can then be packed in bags.

Freeze and pack different herbs separately, making sure the bags are thick enough to prevent other foods in the freezer taking up the flavour. (N.B. Do not substitute two bags for one thick one to protect other foods from any flavour seepage: air will be trapped between the bags and will insulate the food.)

If you want to make ice cubes containing tiny sprigs of mint or a fresh raspberry or strawberry for use in drinks, boil the water first and allow it to cool before use. Boiled water freezes clear and the oxygen is driven off, so there is no danger of enzyme changes taking place.

Vegetable Freezing Chart

VEGETABLE AND PREPARATION	BLANCHING TIME AND PACKING METHOD
Artichokes, globe	
Cut off coarse leaves and stems, remove the 'chokes' and wash thoroughly.	5–7 minutes. Add a few drops of lemon juice to the blanching water. Cool, then drain upside-down before packing in polythene bags.
Artichokes, Jerusalem	
Not worth freezing as a vegetable; better made into soup and frozen.	
Asparagus	
Rinse well, cut off woody stalks and grade according to thickness. Tie in small bundles.	Thin stems: 2 minutes. Thick stems: 4 minutes. Best packed flat in rigid containers.
Beans, broad	
Shell and grade for size. Discard old or shrivelled beans.	Small: 2 minutes. Large: 3 minutes. Open-freeze on trays before packing into polythene bags or pack directly into bags.
Beans, French	
Top, tail and rinse. Leave whole or cut in chunks if you prefer or if the beans are large.	Whole: 3 minutes. Cut: 2 minutes. Open-freeze on trays before packing in polythene bags, or pack directly into bags.
Beans, runner	
Top, tail and string if necessary. Best cut in chunks of 1–2.5 cm (½–1 in). (Beans too finely shredded tend to become limp and flavourless.)	2 minutes. Open-freeze on trays before packing in polythene bags, or pack directly into bags.
Broccoli	
Rinse thoroughly in salted water, then trim leaves and stems, if necessary, and divide into sprigs.	3–4 minutes. Best packed, tops to tails, in rigid containers.

VEGETABLE AND PREPARATION	BLANCHING TIME AND PACKING METHOD
Brussels sprouts	
Grade for size; small to medium-sized firm sprouts are best for freezing. Remove any discoloured outer leaves, then soak for 5 minutes in salted water if dirty.	3 minutes. Open-freeze, if liked, or pack straight into polythene bags or containers.
Carrots	
Choose young, small carrots for freezing. Wash and trim. (After blanching, skin will easily rub off.)	5 minutes. Pack in polythene bags.
Cauliflowers	
Choose firm white cauliflowers for freezing. Break into sprigs and wash well.	3 minutes. Add a few drops of lemon juice to the blanching water. Pack in polythene bags or containers.
Celery	
May be frozen for cooking but not for eating raw. Trim roots and leaves and remove any strings. Scrub and cut into 2.5-cm (1-in) chunks.	5 minutes. Pack in rigid containers and cover with a little of the blanching water.
Courgettes	
Trim the ends and cut into 2.5-cm (1-in) slices. (Can also be frozen after gentle frying in a little butter or oil and quick cooling.)	2 minutes. Pack in polythene bags.
Leeks	
Trim roots and tops and remove tough outside leaves. Wash very thoroughly, then cut into 2.5-cm (1-in) lengths.	2 minutes. Pack in polythene bags or containers.
Mushrooms	
Choose button mushrooms for preference. Wash and trim. (Can also be frozen after gentle frying in butter.)	No blanching needed. Pack in rigid containers

VEGETABLE AND PREPARATION	BLANCHING TIME AND PACKING METHOD
Peas	
Pod and grade.	1 minute. Can be open-frozen if free-running peas are required, or packed straight into polythene bags.
Peppers (red or green)	
Wash, halve and remove membranes and seeds. Slice. (Can also be frozen without blanching.)	3 minutes. Pack in polythene bags.
Potatoes, new	
Use small, even-sized potatoes. Scrape slightly, under-cook and cool.	Pack in polythene bags.
Potatoes, chipped	
Blanch, cool and freeze, ready for subsequent frying, or partly fry, cool and freeze for final frying later.	3 minutes. Pack in polythene bags.
Spinach	
Cut off stems and wash thoroughly. (Drain well before and after blanching.)	2–3 minutes. Pack in small containers.

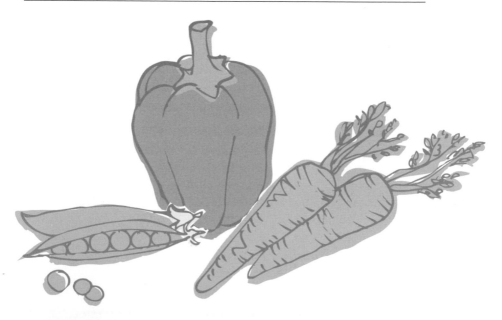

Storage Chart for Frozen Fruit & Vegetables

Frozen food does not keep indefinitely and different types of food can be kept for varying lengths of time. Below are the recommended freezer storage times. All the foods will keep for longer, but their quality and flavour will begin to deteriorate.

Citrus fruit	6 months
Soft fruit	10–12 months
Stoned fruit	skins begin to toughen after 6 months
Fruit purées	10–12 months
Fruit juices	8–10 months
Syrups	9–12 months
Tomatoes, whole or sliced	6 months
Tomatoes, purée	8 months
Vegetables	10–12 months
Vegetable purées	8–10 months
Herbs	6–9 months
Made-up dishes containing sauces	2 months
Made-up dishes containing raw or cooked pastry	1–2 months
Soups	1–2 months

Freezer Recipes

The following recipes offer a few suggestions for freezing vegetables in a made-up dish (for vegetables that are really not suitable for freezing raw, such as Jerusalem artichokes and onions) and ways to use home-frozen fruit and vegetables. Some of the recipes could either be made using frozen vegetables, or made when these vegetables are plentiful so the whole dish is made at once and then frozen. Although the taste would be quite satisfactory, it seems rather pointless to freeze things twice – and it makes extra work for you!

Artichoke Soup

SERVES 5–6
6 large Jerusalem artichokes
1 onion
1–2 stalks celery
25 g (1 oz) butter
1 litre (2 pints) vegetable stock
1 x 5 ml spoon (1 teaspoon) salt
pinch of pepper

Peel and chop the artichokes and onion. Chop the celery. Melt the butter in a saucepan and add the vegetables. Cook gently, covered, for 15 minutes, shaking the pan now and again to prevent sticking. Do not brown the vegetables. Stir in the stock and seasoning and bring to the boil. Cook gently until the vegetables are tender. Liquidize or put through a sieve, cool quickly, pour into a rigid container and freeze.

To serve, thaw the soup completely then re-heat gently. Stir in 150 ml (¼ pint) single cream and serve sprinkled with chopped parsley.

Leeks & Sprouts

Leeks and Brussels sprouts can both be frozen. Leeks must be very thoroughly washed and drained and cut in chunks about 2.5 cm (1 in) long. They should be blanched for 2 minutes in boiling water, drained and cooled quickly, then cooked again until tender. Sprouts do not need to be blanched first: put them in cold water, bring to the boil and cook until just tender.

If frozen in foil dishes, these vegetables can be warmed through in the oven or microwave, then perhaps finished off with a topping of grated cheese and dabs of butter and grilled.

Broccoli with Almonds

This simple yet delicious recipe goes well with trout.

SERVES 4
500 g (1 lb) frozen broccoli
salt
50 g (2 oz) butter
25–50 g (1–2 oz) flaked almonds
few drops of lemon juice

Place the broccoli in a little boiling, salted water. Bring back to the boil and simmer gently until just tender.

Meanwhile, melt the butter in a pan. Add the flaked almonds, sprinkle with a little salt and fry gently until golden brown. Stir in a few drops of lemon juice.

Drain the broccoli and put in a warmed dish. Pour over the almond mixture and serve at once.

Tomato Soup

SERVES 4
750 g (1½ lb) frozen tomatoes
1 onion
50 g (2 oz) butter
600 ml (1 pint) chicken or beef stock
salt and pepper
sugar
150 ml (¼ pint) single cream
1 x 15 ml spoon (1 tablespoon) finely grated orange rind

Chop the tomatoes roughly after thawing slightly to make the chopping easier. Peel and chop the onion. Melt the butter in a pan, add the onion and cook gently until soft. Add the stock and tomatoes and bring to the boil. Season to taste with salt, pepper and a pinch of sugar and simmer for 30 minutes.

Sieve the soup, or liquidize it and pour through a sieve back into the pan. Stir in the cream and re-heat gently but do not allow to boil. Pour the soup into bowls and sprinkle each serving with a little orange rind.

You could also make this soup for freezing. Pour it into rigid containers after liquidizing it. Add the cream and the orange rind after thawing and heating.

Bean Salad

SERVES 4
250 g (8 oz) frozen broad or French beans
250 g (8 oz) frozen peas
2 shallots
olive oil
vinegar
salt and pepper

Cook the frozen beans and peas separately in boiling, salted water until tender. Drain and cool. Mix together. Peel and finely chop the shallots and add to the vegetables. Make a French dressing with olive oil, vinegar and seasoning to taste (a flavoured vinegar is very good in this recipe). Toss the vegetables in the dressing just before serving.

Crispy Spinach

SERVES 4
25 g (1 oz) butter
500 g (1 lb) frozen spinach
4 eggs
50 g (2 oz) coarse stale breadcrumbs
salt and pepper
grated nutmeg

Melt the butter in a pan. Add the spinach and heat through gently, stirring occasionally. Poach the eggs.

When the spinach is really hot, stir in enough breadcrumbs to absorb all excess liquid. Season to taste with salt, pepper and a little nutmeg. Spoon the spinach into a flameproof dish. Make four hollows in the spinach, and slide in the poached eggs. Sprinkle any remaining crumbs on top of the eggs and grill for 1 minute.

Fruit Fool

Choose the quantities of custard and cream according to how extravagant you feel! The larger quantity of cream will make a slightly richer pudding.

SERVES 5–6
600 ml (1 pint} frozen fruit purée (gooseberry, damson
or blackcurrant are all particularly good for this recipe)
125 g (4 oz) caster sugar, if required
300 ml (½ pint) whipping cream
150 ml (¼ pint) custard or 150 ml (¼ pint) whipping cream
300 ml (½ pint) custard

Barely thaw the fruit purée. Add sugar if required, making sure it has completely dissolved. Whip the cream and fold into the purée with the custard. Pour into a serving bowl. Chill in the refrigerator until required.

When making custard for use in a fool, make it a little thicker than the usual pouring consistency. An unbeaten egg white added to the cream before whipping increases the volume of the cream and makes the fool less rich, but in this case you must use double cream.

Ice Cream

A delicious, full-flavoured ice cream can be made from equal quantities of thawed, sweetened fruit purée and whipped cream. Just mix together, pour into a suitable size container and freeze. Sweetened fruit purées also make excellent sauces for vanilla ice cream, steamed sponge puddings and milk puddings.

Raspberry Sorbet

SERVES 4
125 g (4 oz) sugar
300 ml (½ pint) water
1 x 5 ml spoon (1 teaspoon) powdered gelatine
1 x 15 ml spoon (1 tablespoon) lemon juice
150 ml (¼ pint) frozen raspberry purée
1 egg white

Put the sugar and water in a saucepan and heat gently, stirring to dissolve the sugar. Bring to the boil and boil for 5 minutes. Remove from the heat, add the gelatine and stir until dissolved. Add the lemon juice and slightly thawed raspberry purée and mix well. Pour into an ice-cube tray and freeze until semi-solid. Turn into a bowl. Whisk the egg white until stiff and beat into the sorbet. Return to the tray and re-freeze.

This sorbet has a softish texture. Serve it with a few chilled or fresh peaches or strawberries to make a special dessert.

Apple Snow

This is another good use for a frozen fruit purée.

SERVES 6–8
600ml (1 pint) frozen apple purée
1 lemon
125 g (4 oz) caster sugar, if required
2 egg whites

Thaw the purée and heat gently. Grate the rind from the lemon and add to the purée with the sugar, if required. Simmer for a few minutes, then allow to cool.

Whisk the egg whites until stiff and fold into the apple purée. Whisk again until the mixture becomes light and fluffy. Spoon into a dish and chill. Serve with single cream.

Apricot Mousse

Frozen strawberry, raspberry, gooseberry or blackcurrant purées can be used instead of the apricot in this recipe. If doing so, omit the lemon juice and use a little water instead.

SERVES 6–8
600 ml (1 pint) frozen apricot purée
125 g (4 oz) caster sugar (if the purée is not sufficiently sweetened)
12 g (½ oz) powdered gelatine
juice of ½ lemon
3 egg whites
300 ml (½ pint) whipping cream
toasted almonds or hazelnuts

Thaw the purée and, if unsweetened, stir in the caster sugar. Make sure it has dissolved completely. Dissolve the gelatine in the lemon juice and a little water in a bowl over a pan of hot water, then stir into the apricot purée. Whisk the egg whites until stiff and fold into the thickening purée. Whip the cream, reserving a little for decoration, and fold into the mousse. Spoon into a large dish or individual dishes and chill in the refrigerator. Decorate with the reserved cream and a few flaked, toasted almonds or hazelnuts.

Bottling

BOTTLING is probably the modern equivalent of the 'conserve' of the Middle Ages. Then, fruit was cooked in a syrup made from honey, packed into a container and covered with a layer of mutton fat or something similar. The high concentration of sugar, as well as the heat used in the cooking process and the fact that the food was completely sealed, preserved the fruit and enabled it to be kept for a limited period.

Nowadays, with our greater knowledge of the principles of preservation, the process of bottling is comparatively simple, and it is an excellent way of preserving food. The natural flavour and texture of the fruit, in the main, is retained, although the flavour is generally a little sweeter and the fruit will be somewhat softened by the heating process.

Moulds, bacteria, yeasts and the food enzymes can all spoil food but heating to the appropriate temperature in suitable containers and keeping the containers at that temperature for a specified time will destroy the micro-organisms. Secure sealing of bottles is essential so that no other micro-organisms in unsterilized air can enter after the bottles have been packed and processed.

Syrups

Fruit may be bottled in syrup or water. Both are suitable but experience has shown that fruit bottled in a sugar and water syrup and then stored for some weeks or months has a far better flavour and colour than fruit bottled in water. The use of syrup has one main drawback: it can cause the fruit to rise in the bottles, which detracts from the appearance – a particularly important factor if the fruit is being entered for show or competition.

The strength of the syrup can be varied to suit individual tastes and needs but a good average is 250 g (8 oz) sugar to 600 ml (1 pint) water. This gives roughly 50 g (2 oz) sugar per 500 g (1 lb) fruit bottled.

Golden syrup or honey may be used instead of sugar and would be added in similar proportions. Both will alter the flavour of the preserve a little, particularly with delicately flavoured fruit, but you may prefer this.

People with diabetes and slimmers should bottle fruit in water, adding sugar substitutes when the bottle is opened. The fruit will need to be heated before serving to allow the sweetener to penetrate the fruit tissues. If sweetening agents are used to make a syrup for use in bottling, a bitter, unpleasant flavour will develop.

Orange or lemon rind, brandy, liqueurs or whole spices can be added to syrups if wished. It is advisable to strain all syrups through a sieve lined with muslin or fine cotton before use.

Granulated sugar is the best and most economical for use in making the syrup. Add it to half the quantity of water specified in a recipe and stir over low heat until the sugar has dissolved. Bring to the boil and boil for 1 minute, then add the remainder of the water. (This saves time waiting for the syrup to cool sufficiently for use.) Any left-over syrup can be kept in a covered container in the refrigerator for up to a week and used as required.

Equipment

Sterilizing pan Purpose-built sterilizers complete with false bottom and thermometer, and capable of holding up to 6 bottles at a time are available. They are not cheap but will give a lifetime's service. Alternatively, a large deep pan, such as a fish kettle, preserving pan or the base of a pressure cooker used as an open pan can all be used quite satisfactorily. Whatever pan is used, it should be deep enough to contain a false bottom made of folded newspaper, slatted wood or straw, and still take enough water to reach the level of the liquid in the bottles.

Pressure cooker For the pressure-cooker method of sterilizing.

Thermometer Special thermometers for bottling and jam-making, registering up to 110°C/230°F, are available. A sugar thermometer can also be used.

Bottling tongs Not essential, but very helpful when handling hot bottles.

Wooden spoons Long-handled, useful when packing fruit into larger bottles. As an alternative, a clean wooden ruler can be used; or, best of all, carve yourself a 'packing-stick', which is merely a long stick of wood with a rounded end.

Bottles Special bottling jars are produced by several manufacturers. All have metal or glass tops held on by screw bands or spring clips. They are obtainable in various sizes, of which you will probably find the 500-ml (1-lb) or 1-litre (2-lb) sizes the most useful. Although the initial cost is high, the jars will last for years if carefully handled. The metal tops or rubber rings must not be used more than once. (It is also possible to buy hoist or clip-on tops specially made for use with ordinary jam jars.)

Care of Equipment

Store unused jars carefully, to lessen the risk of breakages or chipping, and pack glass lids separately. Screw rings can be removed, washed, thoroughly dried and slightly oiled before storing in a plastic bag to prevent rusting. Unused metal tops with rubber rings attached can be stored in airtight boxes or plastic bags; a little talcum powder rubbed over the rubber rings will help to keep them supple.

At the start of every bottling season, check the equipment, whether old or new.

Check bottle rims for chips or flaws, as this can be the cause of a faulty seal, and check rims of glass lids, if used, for flaws or chips. See that metal rims and tops are not distorted and that spring clips, if used, still 'spring'.

If in doubt about any jar, fill it with water, fit rubber rings and lid with either screw bands or clips and invert the jar on a level surface. If, after 5–10 minutes, there is any sign of leakage, the jar or fittings are suspect and should not be used.

Before use, wash bottles or jars thoroughly in hot water, rinse and leave upside-down to drain. Do not dry jars, particularly if bottling fruit for a competition, as they are much easier to fill when the insides are damp.

For ease in putting rubber rings on bottles, soak in warm water for 10–15 minutes, then dip in boiling water just before use. This makes them supple and easier to manipulate and also sterilizes them.

Choice of Fruit and Preparation

Fruit chosen for bottling should be fresh and just ripe, free from disease and, as far as possible, also free from discoloration. It is not necessary to wash most fruit, unless they are really dirty, in which case they are probably not of good enough quality for bottling. Fruit can be lightly rinsed, if desired. Select and grade fruit for evenness of size.

Apples Cooking varieties rather than dessert apples are best for bottling. Peel, core and cut into rings, halves or quarters. Put straight into lightly salted water – 50 g (2 oz) salt per 4 litres (1 gallon) water – to prevent discoloration. Rinse quickly in cold water before packing in jars.

Apples, pulped A good way of using imperfect, windfall or glut fruit, this also enables more fruit to be preserved in each jar. Peel, core and slice the apples, then stew with a small amount of water, stirring occasionally. Sweeten to taste, if desired. Pour the hot pulp into hot jars and seal. Place the jars in a pan or sterilizer (fitted with a false bottom) of hot water. Bring the water to boiling point and keep at that point for 5 minutes. N.B. This method of sterilizing is only used when bottling *hot* pulps or purées.

Apricots Wash, halve and stone. Pack quickly, cut sides down, in jars before the cut sides discolour. If you like, a few stones may be cracked and the kernels packed with the fruit.

Blackberries Pick over carefully for any leaves, stalks or grubs. Rinse carefully (if you do this too vigorously, you may damage the berries). Drain well before packing into jars.

Blackcurrants String or stalk and remove any green or unripe currants. Wash and drain well before packing into jars.

Cherries Remove stalks, wash and drain well. All varieties of cherries tend to lose colour when bottled (commercial bottled or canned cherries have colouring added). The red Morello usually gives good results, and some of the white-heart varieties give satisfactory results. It is usual to add citric acid to the syrup when bottling cherries, in the proportion of 1 x 5 ml spoon (1 teaspoon) to 2 litres (4 pints).

Damsons Remove stalks and pick over and remove any under-ripe fruit. Wash and drain well before packing into jars.

Gooseberries If preserving in syrup, prick the skins or use a small sharp knife to remove a small slice at either end when topping and tailing. This prevents the gooseberries shrivelling during the bottling process. Wash and drain well before packing into jars.

Loganberries Pick over for any maggoty or under-ripe fruit. Remove hulls, wash and drain before packing.

Peaches Dip in boiling water for ½–1 minute and then dip straight into cold water; the skins will then come off easily. Halve and stone and pack quickly, cut sides down, before the cut surfaces discolour.

Pears Use dessert pears; hard cooking pears are best used in other forms of preservation. Peel and halve the pears and use a teaspoon to remove the cores. Place in salted water – 50 g (2 oz) salt per 4 litres (1 gallon) water – to prevent discoloration. Rinse in cold water and pack and process without any delay. Pears discolour very rapidly, so it is advisable to prepare and bottle in small quantities.

Plums Remove stalks, wash and drain. Plums can be bottled whole or halved; if halved, follow the directions for apricots.

Raspberries As with all soft fruit, raspberries need very careful handling. Remove plugs, and pick over for any damaged or maggoty fruit. Do not rinse unless absolutely necessary.

Redcurrants String or stalk and remove any green or unripe currants. Wash and drain well before packing into jars. Sometimes raspberries and redcurrants are packed together to give a jar of mixed fruit.

Rhubarb (unsoaked) Remove leaves and base, wipe sticks and cut into even lengths suitable for the size of the bottles.

Rhubarb (soaked) This is a more economical method of packing rhubarb. Pour hot sugar syrup over the wiped and chopped-up chunks of rhubarb and leave for 12 hours. Drain the fruit and pack into bottles. Strain the syrup and pour it over fruit.

Bottling Rhubarb

If using hard water when bottling rhubarb, a slight white deposit may occur after processing. This is quite harmless but, if you wish to enter your bottled rhubarb for show or competition, use previously boiled or softened water to make the syrup.

Strawberries (unsoaked) Hull berries and rinse if really necessary, but handle the berries very carefully for they bruise and become 'mashed' very easily. Drain well before packing. Unsoaked fruit shrinks badly during the bottling process.

Strawberries (soaked) Hull, rinse and drain berries. Cover with hot syrup and leave overnight. Pack into bottles and strain the syrup before pouring over the fruit.

Strawberries, soaked or unsoaked, are improved if a little artificial (edible!) red food colouring is added to the syrup. Medium-sized fruit gives best results.

Tomatoes (solid pack) Dip ripe, firm tomatoes, into boiling water for 15–20 seconds, then in cold water so the skins peel off easily. Large tomatoes are usually halved or quartered, but small ones may be packed whole. Pack the fruit tightly in the jars, adding 1 x .2.5 ml spoon (½ teaspoon) each sugar and salt and 1 ml (¼ teaspoon) citric acid or 10 ml (2 teaspoons) lemon juice to each 500-ml (1-lb) jar during the packing. Do not add any liquid.

Tomatoes (in brine) Use small-to-medium ripe but firm tomatoes. Remove stems, wash in cold water and drain. Pack into bottles or jars and cover with brine made from 12 g (½ oz) salt and 5 ml (1 teaspoon) citric acid or 50 ml (2 fl oz) lemon juice to 1 litre (2 pints) water.

Packing the Bottles

Soft Fruit

Pack as tightly as possible in layers without squashing and add syrup about every 4–5 layers. This helps to give a better proportion of fruit to syrup with soft fruit. If using jars with rubber rings, dip the ring in boiling water before placing on the rim of the bottle. Check carefully that no seeds (such as raspberry or tomato) are on or under the ring, as this would prevent an airtight seal. Just before putting on the lids, clips or screw bands, give the bottles a sharp jerk to remove as many air bubbles as possible. Check to see whether any more syrup is required before covering.

Hard Fruit

Pack tightly and fill with syrup after packing. Pour the syrup down the side of the jar and give the bottles a sharp jerk before covering to remove as many air bubbles as possible. Add a little more syrup if necessary.

Before any bottles of fruit are sterilized, loosen the screw bands a quarter of a turn to allow air and steam to escape, otherwise there is a danger that the bottles will burst.

Methods of Sterilizing

There are four methods of sterilizing bottled fruit:

1. The slow water-bath method (very reliable, but a thermometer is required).

2. The quick water-bath method (thermometer can be helpful but it is not essential).

3. The oven method.

4. Pressure cooking (quick, but very easy to over-cook the fruit).

Slow water-bath

You can use either a special sterilizer, complete with false bottom and fitted thermometer, or a really deep fish kettle, saucepan or even a small boiler with a makeshift false bottom for this method (see page 99). Fill the bottles with prepared fruit, cover with cold syrup up to the rim, then put on the tops. If using screw bands, loosen them a quarter turn.

Place the bottles on the false bottom, making certain they do not touch each other or the sides of the pan. Fill the pan with cold water until the bottles are completely covered. If this is impossible, the water should reach the shoulders of the bottles and the pan must have a tight-fitting lid. Heat slowly, taking about 1 hour to reach 55°C/130°F. Allow a further 30–35 minutes to reach the recommended temperature for the contents (check the processing chart on page 152).

When the bottles have been at the recommended temperature for the specified time, switch off the heat. Remove the bottles one at a time with bottling tongs or a good thick cloth. If using a cloth, take out a little of the hot water first.

As each bottle is removed, place it on a wooden surface, if possible (a bread board is useful), and immediately tighten the screw-band. This is *essential* to hold the lid in position until a vacuum is formed by the cooling of the contents. Stand and leave to cool. Check the screw bands, screwing down again if necessary. This method can be used without a thermometer but greater control is possible with a thermometer. If entering bottles for show or competition, where appearance is important, it is worthwhile investing in one. N.B. Do not attempt to hurry this process by cutting down on the time taken. Not only is it essential that the heat has sufficient time to penetrate to the centre of the fruit, but raising the temperature too quickly can cause the fruit to rise in the bottles.

Quick water-bath
As in the slow water-bath method, use a deep pan or sterilizer, fitted with a false bottom. Pack the prepared fruit and hot syrup into warm bottles up to the brim. Cover the bottles (loosening them a quarter turn, if using screw-bands) and place in the pan.

Pour in *warm* water until the bottles are submerged, or until the water comes at least to shoulder level. Heat slowly so that the water reaches simmering point (88°C/190°F) in 25–30 minutes. Continue simmering for the recommended time (check the processing chart on page 152).

Oven method, dry pack

Pre-heat the oven to 130°C, 250°F/Gas ½ (it is a good idea to check the oven temperature with an oven thermometer). Pack the prepared fruit into the bottles and place the lids, if used, on top. Otherwise, cover with old saucers or plates. Put the bottles on a piece of thick cardboard or on a roasting tin covered with newspaper, in the centre of the oven. Good circulation of hot air is necessary, so allow 5 cm (2 in) between each bottle, and between the bottles and the sides of the oven. Check the processing chart on page 153 for time required according to the fruit being used.

If processing fruit of different sizes, for example large and small damsons, place bottles of larger fruit near the sides of the oven, and smaller fruit in the centre.

The success of oven bottling of fruit depends greatly on filling and sealing the bottles as quickly as possible after removal from the oven. So, when the processing time is completed, remove the bottles *one at a time* from the oven and fill to the brim with boiling syrup or water. If the fruit has shrunk during its time in the oven, fill with fruit from one of the other bottles before adding the boiling liquid. If using rubber rings, have them ready in a bowl of boiling water. As with the previous methods, check screw bands as the bottles cool and tighten if necessary.

Oven method, wet pack

In this method, the bottles are packed and filled with boiling syrup or water before placing in the oven. This avoids the problems of handling hot bottles and boiling liquids, but the fruit is more liable to break up.

Pre-heat the oven to 150°C, 300°F/Gas 2. Again, it is a good idea to check the oven temperature with a thermometer. Pack warm bottles with fruit and fill with boiling syrup or water. Put on rubber rings and covers. If using rubber rings, it is often easier to put these in position before filling the bottles but check to see they are properly in position before putting on the tops. Do not put screw-bands on until the bottles are removed from the oven.

Put the filled bottles on a baking sheet or tin lined with newspaper (in case any liquid boils out during processing). As with the previous method, a good circulation of hot air is necessary, so allow 5 cm (2 in) between bottles, and between the bottles and the sides of the oven. Check the processing chart for times (see page 153).

Remove the bottles *one at a time* from the oven and screw down or spring clip. Leave to cool, wipe if sticky, and tighten screw bands if necessary.

The oven method of bottling does not always produce bottles with the best appearance, as temperatures vary from oven to oven, and from one part of the oven to another. This is why, if at all possible, the oven temperature should be checked with a thermometer at the *centre* of the oven, which is where the bottles should then be placed. (To make sure the bottles are at the true centre of the oven, remember that the shelf on which they stand will be *below* the centre of the oven.) In any event, this method is perfectly satisfactory for fruit that will mainly be used for stewing or for pies and tarts.

For fruits that discolour easily in the air, such as pears, use the wet-pack method rather than the dry. If using tall or large jars of over 1 litre (2 lb), neither oven method is recommended, as the fruit at the top will be cooked before the bottom and centre are sterilized.

Pressure-cooker method

This is very quick, and economical on fuel. However soft fruits, in particular, may end up looking a little over-cooked. The cooker must be deep enough to take the bottles or jars and must be fitted with a false bottom as previously described. It must also be capable of maintaining a steady 'low' pressure.

Pack the fruit into warm bottles and fill with boiling syrup or water to within 2.5 cm (1 in) of the rim. Fit rubber rings, lids and clips. If using screw-bands, these should be loosened a quarter turn. Pour boiling water into the cooker to a depth of 2.5 cm (1 in). Place the bottles on the false bottom, checking that they do not touch each other, or the sides of the pan. Pads of newspaper will help to keep them apart. Put the lid on the pan, with the vent open, and heat until steam appears. Close the vent and bring the pressure up to 'low'. The time taken from the start of heating until pressure is reached should be not less than 5 nor more than 10 minutes. Check the processing chart on page 153 for the time necessary to maintain pressure.

Remove the pan from the heat and *leave for 10 minutes* before opening and removing the bottles (the sterilizing process is continuing during this 10 minutes). Any screw-bands should be tightened when the bottles are removed from the pan. Check again as the bottles cool.

Testing the seal

Whatever method of processing is used, allow the bottles to cool completely afterwards, preferably for 12–24 hours. At the end of the cooling period, test for sealing. To do this, remove the screw bands or spring clips and lift each bottle by the lid only. Do this over a bowl or the sink in case of accidents. If the bottle has sealed properly, the lid will hold. If the lid comes off, examine the bottle to see if you can discover the reason – chipped rims, perished rubber rings or seals, or even a seed on or under the ring.

If you can rectify the fault, the fruit may be re-processed, although the quality will be affected. It is better to use the fruit straight away, as if from a freshly opened bottle.

Storage

Wipe the bottles to remove any stickiness and label with the contents, type of liquid used and date. If the bottles are properly sealed, it is not necessary to replace the screw-bands and spring clips. If you prefer to store bottles complete with screw-bands, rub a little oil around the inside. This helps to prevent rust and makes for ease of opening later on. Spring clips are weakened if they are left on bottles for months at a time, so are better removed.

Further suggestions

Soft fruit such as strawberries, raspberries and blackberries can be rolled in caster sugar and then packed tightly into bottles. *No* liquid is used and either of the water-bath methods may be used for processing. The one drawback to these methods is that the fruit shrinks considerably; the flavour is delicious, however. Certain fruit may be bottled in brandy – damsons, peaches, pears and cherries are particularly good. Prepare them as for the slow water-bath method (damsons should be pricked all over with a stainless steel fork first to allow the flavoured syrup to penetrate). Make a heavy syrup, 350 g (12 oz) sugar to 600 ml (1 pint) water. Add up to an equal quantity of brandy. Pack fruit into bottles, fill up with the cold brandy syrup and check the processing chart on page 152 for recommended times.

Things That Can Go Wrong

• Too rapid heating, or over-heating, can cause the fruit to rise or sink in the bottles.

• A combination of heavy syrup and too rapid heating can cause the fruit to rise. This is not something that can be corrected after processing but, unless the bottle is wanted for show purposes, it does not really matter.

• Mould can be caused by insufficient sterilizing, or by a poor seal. The affected fruit should be discarded. Even though some of the lower fruit might look all right, the mould growth may have reduced the acidity content, allowing certain harmful bacteria to grow.

• Fermentation may be caused by using over-ripe fruit or insufficient sterilizing.

• Poor colour and flavour may be caused by over-cooking, or using unripe fruit.

Hints for Exhibitors

• Wide-mouthed bottles are much easier to pack when producing bottled fruit for show or competition.

• Grade fruit for size and degree of ripeness before packing; this helps to give a uniform appearance.

• Check the schedule to see whether the fruit should be in syrup or water.

- The label should state the contents, whether the contents are bottled in light or heavy syrup, or in water, and the date.

- Clips and screw-bands should be removed and any stickiness wiped from the top of the bottle.

- Rub the outside of the bottles with a soft cloth sprinkled with a few drops of methylated spirits. This removes finger marks and makes the glass sparkle. Use a little metal polish on metal tops and finish with a soft rag or duster.

Processing Chart for Bottling Fruit

Water-bath methods
These times and temperatures apply to bottles of up to 1 litre (2 lb). If 2-litre (4-lb) bottles are used, add 5 minutes; for 3-litre (6-lb) bottles, add 10 minutes. If processing solid-pack tomatoes, double the above times.

When using a slow water-bath method, sterilizing times start from the moment the water reaches the required temperature – as specified on the chart. When using the quick water-bath method, sterilizing times start from the moment the water reaches simmering point.

Note that the temperatures on the chart apply only to the slow water-bath method. For correct temperatures for other methods of sterilizing, see individual instructions in the main text.

Oven methods
The times apply to bottles of up to 2 litres (4 lb).

Pressure-cooker method
Raise from hot to 5-lb pressure in 5–10 minutes. Maintain at this pressure for the number of minutes indicated in the chart, then leave to cool for 10 minutes before opening the cooker.

Water bath (Slow method)

Fruit	Temperature	Sterilizing time in minutes
Apples (slices)	74°C/165°F	10
Apples (solid pack)	82°C/180°F	15
Apricots (halved)	82°C/180°F	15
Apricots (whole)	82°C/180°F	15
Blackberries	74°C/165°F	10
Cherries	82°C/180°F	15
Currants	74°C/165°F	10
Damsons	82°C/180°F	15
Gooseberries (for pies)	74°C/165°F	10
Gooseberries (for dessert)	82°C/180°F	15
Loganberries	74°C/165°F	10
Peaches (halved)	82°C/180°F	15
Pears	88°C/190°F	30
Plums (whole)	82°C/180°F	15
Plums (halved)	82°C/180°F	15
Raspberries	74°C/l65°F	10
Rhubarb (for pies)	74°C/l65°F	10
Rhubarb (for dessert)	82°C/180°F	15
Strawberries (unsoaked)	74°C/165°F	10
Strawberries (soaked in syrup)	82°C/180°F	15
Tomatoes (solid-pack)	88°C/190°F	40
Tomatoes (in brine)	88°C/190°F	30

Bottling fruit in the oven (Quick method)

Sterilizing time in minutes	Wet pack in minutes	Dry pack in minutes	Pressure cooker in minutes
2	30–40	*not recommended*	1
20	50–60	*not recommended*	3–4
20	50–60	*not recommended*	3–4
10	40–50	*not recommended*	1
2	30–40	45–55	1
10	40–50	55–70	1
2	30–40	45–55	1
10	40–50	55–70	1
2	30–40	45–55	1
10	40–50	55–70	1
2	30–40	45–55	1
20	50–60	*not recommended*	3–4
40	60–70	*not recommended*	5
10	40–50	*not recommended*	1
20	50–60	*not recommended*	3–4
2	30–40	45–55	1
2	30–40	45–55	1
10	40–50	55–70	1
2	30–40	45–55	1
20	50–60	*not recommended*	3–4
50	70–80	*not recommended*	15
40	60–70	80–100	5

Pickling, Drying Salting & Crystallizing

Pickling

PICKLING is a method of preserving vegetables and fruit, and is an excellent way of using gluts or bumper crops. It is comparatively easy to produce a range of pickles for use all the year round, and they can provide a welcome addition to snack meals, or cold meat and salads, as well as providing additional flavouring to goulash and curries.

Equipment

Saucepans Aluminium or stainless steel.

Knives Stainless steel.

Bowls Large earthenware or plastic.

Grater Stainless steel, useful if using block salt.

Spoons Wooden and perforated.

Sieves Nylon or stainless steel.

Muslin For tying up whole spices.

Scales Metric and imperial.

Jars or bottles Any glass jar or bottle is suitable provided it has, or can be equipped with, the correct lid.

Airtight lids With any preserve containing vinegar, it is vitally important that the tops are vinegar-resistant and airtight. Vinegar will corrode metal and a poor seal will allow vinegar to evaporate and cause the pickle to shrink. Lids or tops *must* be plastic or plastic-coated to prevent vinegar corroding the metal. If metal tops are used, fit discs of vinegar-proof ceresin paper within the lids (obtainable from most chemists). An alternative cover can be made from cotton squares dipped in paraffin wax and tied down.

Vinegar and Spices

All types of pickle, whether raw or cooked, sweetened or unsweetened, are preserved by the action of the acetic acid in vinegar. It is important that good vinegar is used for pickling, with an acetic acid content of at least 5 per cent. This is not always stated on the bottle, so, if you have any doubts, always enquire.

Generally speaking, bulk or draught vinegars, sold loose, are of a lower strength, and are not recommended for pickling. Malt vinegar can be bought in its natural brown colour and also as white distilled vinegar. Either can be used, but white is normally used where a pale-coloured pickle is required.

White wine and cider vinegar are suitable for pickling but they are more expensive and their more delicate flavours can be overwhelmed in a strong pickle.

Spiced vinegars can be bought but they are easily made and offer opportunities for individual tastes and ideas. They are at their best if the spices are allowed to steep in the unheated vinegar for 6–8 weeks before the vinegar is used. The vinegar must be tightly covered during the steeping process. Strain when required for use.

If spiced vinegar is required for use at short notice, the vinegar and spices should be put in a heatproof basin, and the basin stood over a

saucepan of water. The basin must be covered with a plate, otherwise much of the flavour will be lost. Bring the water in the saucepan to the boil, then remove it from the heat. Allow the spices to steep in the warm vinegar for 2–3 hours. Strain and cool.

Use whole rather than ground spices when spicing vinegar, and tie them in a muslin bag before immersing in the vinegar. Ground spices tend to produce a cloudy vinegar, even with careful straining, and, while this may not matter for home use, pickles entered in shows or competitions will be marked down if they are cloudy.

Generally speaking, cold vinegar gives better results when pickling vegetables that should be served crisp, such as onions or cabbage, and hot vinegar is better with softer pickles, such as plums or walnuts.

Suggested Quantities for Spicing Vinegar

These suggested quantities are sufficient for about 1–2 kg (2–4 lb) fruit.

For mild flavour:
1 litre (2 pints) malt vinegar
6 g (¼ oz) each cinnamon bark, whole cloves, blade mace, allspice
a few peppercorns

For a hotter flavour:
1 litre (2 pints) malt vinegar
25 g (1 oz) each mustard seed and allspice
12 g (½ oz) each whole cloves and peppercorns
6 g (¼ oz) each dried root ginger and dried chillies

For sweet and fruit pickles:
1 litre (2 pints) wine, distilled or malt vinegar
1 kg (2 lb) sugar, brown if using malt vinegar, white if using distilled
*   or wine vinegar*
1 x 15 ml spoon (1 tablespoon) each whole allspice, whole cloves
*   and coriander seeds or dried root ginger*
½ cinnamon stick
4 mace blades

Dissolve the sugar in the vinegar, add the spices wrapped in muslin and leave to steep for 6–8 weeks, tightly covered. If required at short notice, spiced vinegar can be made quickly in a basin over a pan of hot water.

Ready-mixed spices are available at many shops. These are useful, as extra spices can be added, if wished, to suit individual taste. However, such packs vary enormously in flavour and it is not always easy to judge just what each one contains. It is therefore preferable to use individual spices when at all possible, as you then have control over the flavour and can adapt it to your taste. Always buy spices from shops that have a fairly rapid turnover, to ensure freshness.

Note In all the pickle recipes given on the following pages, the yield will correspond approximately to the total amount of vegetables or fruit used. In each case, make as much – or as little – as you like, according to your family's taste and requirements.

Vegetable Pickles

Preparation of Vegetables

Use young fresh vegetables and wash and drain them well, removing any damaged portions or tough stalks. Chop, shred or leave whole, according to the recipe. They are then ready for brining or dry salting – processes which extract some of the water from the vegetables.

Use cooking or vacuum-packed salt or block salt if available. Table salt has additives to prevent it going lumpy and tends to make the pickle cloudy. Iodized salt is not suitable, as it has a pronounced flavour.

If the vegetables are to be brined, use a solution of 500 g (1 lb) salt to 4.5 litres (1 gallon) water. Cover the prepared vegetables with this brine and place a plate or lid on top to keep the vegetables under the liquid as much as possible.

For the dry salt method, layer the vegetables with salt in a large bowl, finishing with a layer of salt.

Times for brining or salting are given in each recipe. After brining or salting, rinse the vegetables well under cold running water and drain thoroughly.

Suitable Vegetables for Pickling

Beans, runner or French
Beetroot
Cabbage, red or white
Cauliflower
Cucumber
Gherkins
Onions
Shallots
Walnuts
or combinations such as bean, marrow and onion.

Bottling Vegetable Pickles

Cold Pickling
Pack the prepared (brined and rinsed) vegetables, such as cauliflower, cabbage, cucumber, beans or onions, into clean jars. Leave a headspace of roughly 2.5 cm (1 in). Tip the jar and drain off any water that may have collected at the bottom. Fill with spiced vinegar, covering the contents with at least 12 mm (½ in) of vinegar. Cover with airtight, vinegar-proof lids.

Hot Pickling
Cook the vegetables and, while still hot, pack them into hot jars. Cover with spiced vinegar or sauce, to a depth of at least 12 mm (½ in). Cover with airtight, vinegar-proof lids.

Fruit Pickles

Preparation of Fruit

Fruit for pickling does not require brining or salting. Use only fresh, sound fruit that is just ripe.

If pickling whole fruit, such as damsons or crab apples, prick all over with a silver or stainless steel fork to prevent them shrivelling during the pickling process.

Suitable Fruit for Pickling

Apricots
Blackberries
Crab apples
Damsons
Gooseberries
Lemons
Oranges
Peaches
Pears
Plums

Put the sweetened, spiced vinegar in a saucepan and add the fruit. Simmer until tender. Remove the fruit with a perforated spoon and pack into hot, clean jars, leaving about 2.5 cm (1 in) headspace. Boil the vinegar rapidly, uncovered, until it is reduced by one-third. Fill the jars with the hot, syrupy vinegar, covering the fruit by at least 12 mm (½ in). Cover with airtight, vinegar-proof lids.

Any surplus vinegar should be kept in a covered jar, because some pickled fruit – pears, for example – will absorb more vinegar than others, and the jars may require topping up.

Storage

All pickles, properly sealed, should be stored in a dry, cool and dark place. Most pickles benefit by being left to mature for 6–8 weeks.

Pickled Cabbage

red or white cabbage
cooking salt
spiced vinegar

Choose firm, fresh cabbages. Remove any discoloured leaves, cut into quarters and wash well. Cut away the tough inner stalk and shred the cabbage. Layer in a basin with salt, ending with a layer of salt. Leave for 24 hours, then rinse thoroughly in cold water and drain well. Pack into bottles and cover with cold spiced vinegar. Cover at once. Ready for use after 1 week, but loses its essential crispness after 10–12 weeks storage.

Pickled Cauliflower

If you use distilled vinegar in this recipe, it will help to keep the cauliflower's natural colour.

4 large or 6 medium cauliflowers
500 g (1 lb) cooking salt
4.5 litres (1 gallon) water
spiced vinegar

Choose firm fresh cauliflowers. Trim and break into small florets. Make a brine with the salt and water and steep the florets in the brine for 24 hours. Rinse in cold water, drain well and pack into jars. Cover with cold spiced vinegar and seal. Ready for use after 6 weeks.

Pickled Cucumber

cucumbers
cooking salt
spiced vinegar

Wash the cucumbers, wipe dry, but do not peel unless you think they might be bitter. Cut into bite-size chunks or slices and layer with salt in a basin, finishing with a layer of salt. Leave for 24 hours, then rinse thoroughly in cold water and drain well. Pack into bottles and cover with cold spiced vinegar. Cover at once and leave for 4 weeks before using.

Pickled Onions

Small shallots may be pickled in the same way as pickling onions.

3 kg (6 lb) pickling onions
500 g (1 lb) salt
4. 5 litres (1 gallon) water
approx. 1 litre (2 pints) spiced vinegar

Use small, even-sized onions if possible. Make a brine from the salt and water, and soak the unpeeled onions in it for 12 hours. Drain, peel and soak in a similar quantity of fresh brine for 24–36 hours. Use a plate or something similar to keep the onions below the surface of the brine.

Drain the onions thoroughly, pack into bottles and cover with cold spiced vinegar. Cover at once and leave at least 2 months before using.

Tips for Pickled Onions

• 1 x 5 ml spoon (1 teaspoon) of sugar may be added to each jar of onions; this is a matter of individual taste.

• If any small yellow spots appear on your pickled onions after some time in storage, do not worry. This is a perfectly harmless substance, and does not affect the onions eating quality. If packed in hot vinegar (which will not soften the onions) these spots are unlikely to appear.

Pickled Gherkins

approx. 1.5 kg (3 lb) gherkins
500 g (1 lb) cooking salt
4.5 litres (1 gallon) water
spiced vinegar

Wash the gherkins and prick lightly with a stainless steel fork. Make a brine from the salt and water and soak the gherkins in this for 72 hours. Drain and pack into warm bottles. Cover with boiling spiced vinegar and cover tightly. Leave in a warm room for 24 hours.

Drain off the vinegar and bring it to the boil again. Pour the boiling vinegar back over the gherkins, seal and keep in a warm room for a further 24 hours. Repeat the draining and boiling process once again, at the end of which the gherkins should be a good overall green. Add more vinegar, if necessary, and seal bottles. Ready for eating after 6 weeks

Pickled Walnuts

Use immature green nuts, picked in June or early July. After this, the shells begin to harden and the spiced vinegar will not penetrate and soften the shell, so that there will be hard pieces in the resultant pickle. Always wear rubber gloves when pickling walnuts as the stain is very difficult to remove, and virtually has to wear off the skin.

green walnuts
cooking salt
spiced vinegar

Prick the walnuts with a steel knitting or darning needle. Discard any nuts that have any hard patches at the end opposite the stalk (this is where the shell starts to develop). Make a brine, using 125 g (4 oz) salt and 1 litre (2 pints) water to each 1 kg (2 lb) walnuts, and soak the nuts for 3–4 days. Drain, cover with fresh brine, and leave for 1 week.

Drain thoroughly and spread out on a large tray or dish. Leave uncovered on a sunny window ledge for 24–48 hours, by which time the nuts will have turned black. Pack them into clean jars and cover with cold spiced vinegar. Cover at once and leave at least 6–8 weeks before using.

Sweet Pickled Walnuts

Sweet pickled walnuts are prepared in the same way as ordinary pickled walnuts, but covered with hot sweet spiced vinegar as for fruit pickles.

Pickled Carrots

1 kg (2 lb) young carrots
600 ml (1 pint) distilled white vinegar
300 ml (½ pint) water
250 g (8 oz) white sugar
50 g (2 oz) whole mixed pickling spices

Wash, trim and scrape the carrots. Simmer in water for 10 minutes, then drain. Put the vinegar, water and sugar in a saucepan; tie the spices in muslin and add to the pan. Bring to the boil, stirring until the sugar has dissolved and simmer for 10 minutes. Add the carrots and cook for 15 minutes, or until tender. Remove the bag of spices. Pack the carrots into hot jars and cover with the boiling vinegar. Cover at once and keep for 3–4 weeks before using.

Pickled Mushrooms

500 g (1 lb) young mushrooms
1 small onion or shallot
1 x 5 ml spoon (1 teaspoon) salt
1 x 5 ml spoon (1 teaspoon) ground ginger
pinch ground black pepper
spiced vinegar

Wash the mushrooms and trim the stalks but do not peel. Quarter any large mushrooms. Peel and slice the onion or shallot and place in a saucepan with the mushrooms and salt, ginger and pepper. Barely cover with vinegar, cover with a tight-fitting lid and cook slowly until the mushrooms are tender – about 45 minutes. (The mushrooms will shrink during this process.) Lift out the mushrooms with a perforated spoon and pack into hot jars. Cover with the strained hot vinegar. Cover at once. The mushrooms will be ready for use in 4 weeks.

Onion, Cauliflower, Cucumber & Runner Bean Pickle

Any combination of these vegetables may be used, depending on what you have available.

onions, cauliflower, cucumber and runner beans
cooking salt
spiced vinegar
dried red chillies

Peel the onions (silverskin are very good in this pickle, or small shallots). Wash the cauliflower and break into small florets Wash the cucumber and chop into 12-mm (½-in) chunks. Wash the runner beans, string if necessary and chop into 2.5-cm (1-in) lengths. Mix all the vegetables together, then layer in a bowl with salt. Leave for 48 hours.

Rinse in cold water and drain thoroughly. Pack a good mixture of vegetables into each jar, add a chilli to each jar and cover with cold spiced vinegar. Cover at once and keep for 8 weeks before using.

Pickled Jerusalem Artichokes

artichokes
cooking salt
water
spiced vinegar

Wash and scrape the artichokes. For each 250 g (8 oz) artichokes, put 25 g (1 oz) salt and 600 ml (1 pint) water in a saucepan. Add the artichokes and bring to the boil. Simmer until tender. Drain and, when cold, pack into jars. Fill with cold spiced vinegar. Cover at once. Ready for use in 8–10 weeks.

Pickled Eggs

Try to use eggs that are about 48 hours old for this recipe.

12 fresh eggs
spiced malt or white vinegar
2 blades of mace

Hard-boil the eggs for 10 minutes, giving them an occasional gentle stir during the first few minutes. This helps to centralize the yolks. Plunge immediately into plenty of cold water to prevent a black ring forming round the yolks.

When the eggs are cool, shell them carefully and pack loosely into glass or stone jars. Do not pack too tightly because if the eggs stick together they will have a spotty or mottled look. Cover with cold spiced vinegar, adding 2 blades of mace to each 12 eggs. Seal the jars at once and keep the eggs for 3 weeks before using.

Pickled Eggs in Shows

Although pickled eggs are delicious and one of the most popular pickles, they should not be entered in shows, unless the schedule specifically allows their inclusion.

Piccalilli

Any combination of vegetables may be used, depending on what is available, with either a mild or hot sauce. Choose from cauliflower, courgettes, pickling onions or shallots, marrow, cucumber, French beans, celery and peppers.

500 g (1 lb) cooking salt to every 3 kg (6 lb)
prepared vegetables

Layer the prepared vegetables with the salt in a large bowl and cover with a plate to ensure the vegetables really steep in the salt. Leave for 24 hours. Rinse and drain thoroughly.

Mild sweet sauce
1 x 15 ml spoon (1 tablespoon) turmeric
4 x 5 ml spoons (4 teaspoons) dry mustard
4 x 5 ml spoons (4 teaspoons) ground ginger
250 g (8 oz) sugar
1.5 litres (3 pints) distilled vinegar
50 g (2 oz) cornflour

Hot sharp sauce
1 x 15 ml spoon (1 tablespoon) turmeric
8 x 5 ml spoons (8 teaspoons) dry mustard
8 x 5 ml spoons (8 teaspoons) ground ginger
175 g (6 oz) sugar
1 litre (2 pints) distilled vinegar
25 g (1 oz) cornflour

Put the turmeric, mustard, ginger, sugar and all but 3 x 15 ml spoons (3 tablespoons) of the vinegar in a saucepan. Mix well. Add the vegetables, bring to the boil and simmer gently for 15–20 minutes, testing occasionally. The degree of crispness or tenderness of the vegetables is a matter for individual taste, but do not overcook them.

When ready, remove the vegetables with a perforated spoon and pack into hot jars. Dissolve the cornflour in the reserved vinegar and stir into the vinegar mixture in the pan. Bring to the boil and boil for 3 minutes, stirring continuously. Pour the sauce over the vegetables and cover at once. Ready for use in 6 weeks.

Pickled Beetroot

This is an excellent way of using the 'thinnings' from a row of beetroot.

beetroot
spiced vinegar

Wash beetroot carefully, without rubbing the skin, and cook gently until tender: 45–90 minutes, depending on size. Allow to cool, then rub off the skins. If using large beetroot, cut into slices approx. 6 mm (¼ in) thick or into cubes. Pack into jars and cover with cold spiced vinegar.

Beetroot pickle tends to lose colour if kept longer than 6 months, but if you use boiling spiced vinegar the storage life will be lengthened.

Showing Piccalilli

If entering piccalilli for show or competition, use a clean flat piece of wood to remove any air pockets in the filled jars. Slide the wood down the sides of the jar, re-positioning the vegetables and allowing sauce to fill the spaces between.

Pickled Beans

500 g (1 lb) firm young beans
300 ml (½ pint) boiling water
125 g (4 oz) onion
300 ml (½ pint) cider vinegar, or mixture of vinegar and dry cider
125 g (4 oz) sugar
1 x 5 ml spoon (1 teaspoon) salt
2 x 5 ml spoons (2 teaspoons) dill seeds
pinch red pepper
pinch cayenne pepper

Top and tail the beans, and cook whole in the boiling water till just tender, but still a little crisp. Chop or mince the onion, and add with all remaining ingredients to the vinegar. Bring to the boil, stirring until sugar has dissolved, and boil for 3 minutes.

Drain the beans and pack into warm jars. Pour the hot vinegar over them, giving jars a slight twist to disperse any air bubbles. Cover, and keep for 6–8 weeks before using.

Mexican Pickle

This is a hot one – you will find a little goes a long way!

600 ml (1 pint) white vinegar
1 x 15 ml spoon (1 tablespoon) dried ground chillies
1 x 15 ml spoon (1 tablespoon) mustard powder
1 x 15 ml spoon (1 teaspoon) grated horseradish
1 x 15 ml spoon (1 teaspoon) salt
500 g (1 lb) green tomatoes
2 green peppers
250 g (8 oz) onion

Add the spices and salt to the vinegar, bring to boil and simmer for 9–10 minutes. Wash and chop the tomatoes and wash, de-seed and finely chop the peppers. Peel and chop the onion. Mix the vegetables well together with the horseradish and pack into warm jars. Pour boiling spiced vinegar over the pickle and cover. Ready for use in 6 weeks.

Sweet Pepper Pickle

500 g (1 lb) red peppers
500 g (1 lb) green peppers
piece of dried root ginger
3 chillies
12 peppercorns
350 g (12 oz) onions
125 g (4 oz) white sugar
1 x 2.5 ml spoon (½ teaspoon) ordinary or garlic salt
600 ml (1 pint) white vinegar

Wash the peppers, de-seed and chop. Blanch in boiling water for 2 minutes, then allow to drain. Bruise the ginger and tie with the chillies and peppercorns in a muslin bag. Put in a pan with the sugar, salt and vinegar. Bring to boil, stirring until sugar has dissolved. Add the blanched peppers and peeled and chopped onion to the pan and cook gently, according to degree of tenderness or crispness required. Remove with a perforated spoon and pack into jars. Remove the bag of spices from the pan, and pour hot vinegar over pickle in the jars and cover. Ready for use in 6 weeks.

Apple & Onion Pickle

Add a chilli to each jar, if you want to pep this up a bit!

1 kg (2 lb) cooking or dessert apples
500 g (1 lb) onions
1 litre (2 pints) white vinegar
1 x 15 ml spoon (1 tablespoon) salt
25 g (1 oz) peppercorns

Peel and core the apples and peel the onions. Cut both into bite-size pieces, and put the apples into slightly salted water until you are ready to use them. This will prevent them discolouring. Boil the vinegar, salt and peppercorns. Pack mixed onion and apple into warm jars, and pour the slightly cooled vinegar over them. Cover the jars and keep for 3 weeks before use.

Pickled Apricots

1 kg (2 lb) fresh apricots
600 ml (1 pint) sweet spiced vinegar, preferably made with white or wine vinegar

Halve the apricots and remove the stones. Heat the vinegar and add the fruit. Simmer gently until tender but not mushy. Remove the fruit from the pan with a perforated spoon and pack into hot jars. Boil the vinegar rapidly for 5–7 minutes to reduce. Pour over the fruit and cover at once. Ready for use in 4 weeks.

Fruit Pickles for Competitions

When packing halved fruits, such as apricots, peaches and plums, pack cut sides down for an attractive appearance.

Pickled Damsons I

Try small to medium-sized plums instead of damsons here.

2 kg (4 lb) damsons
1 litre (2 pints) sweet spiced vinegar

Wash the damsons, remove the stalks and pat dry. Prick with a stainless steel fork or skewer. Put the vinegar in a saucepan and add the damsons. Bring to the boil and simmer gently until soft but still whole. Remove the damsons with a perforated spoon and pack carefully into hot jars. Reduce the vinegar by one-third with fast-boiling, then pour over the damsons. Cover at once. Ready for use in 8 weeks.

Pickled Damsons II

If you do not have spiced vinegar ready, try this recipe.

1 kg (2 lb) damsons
piece of dried root ginger
pared rind of ½ lemon
piece of cinnamon stick
1–2 blades mace
4–6 cloves
300 ml (½ pint) white vinegar
500 g (1 lb) white sugar

Remove the stalks from the damsons, then rinse and drain the fruit. Bruise the ginger and tie with the other spices and the lemon rind in a muslin bag. Put in a pan with the vinegar and sugar. Bring to the boil, stirring until the sugar has dissolved. Add the damsons to the pan and simmer gently until tender but still unbroken. Remove the fruit with a perforated spoon and pack carefully into jars. Reduce the liquid in the pan by fast-boiling for 5 minutes, then pour over the damsons and cover. Ready for use in 4 weeks.

Year-round Pickle

A spoonful of this pickle is delicious added to a curry.

250 g (8 oz) prunes
125 g (4 oz) dates
250 g (8 oz) dried apricots
250 g (8 oz) apples, dried or fresh
1 litre (2 pints) spiced vinegar
250 g (8 oz) sugar, brown or white

Soak all the dried fruit overnight in cold water to cover. Next day, drain well and place in a saucepan with a little of the spiced vinegar. Simmer gently until tender. If using fresh apples, add at this stage, either in quarters or thick slices.

In another pan, bring the sugar and remaining vinegar to the boil, stirring to dissolve the sugar. Boil for 15 minutes. Add the boiling vinegar to the pan of fruit and simmer for 3–5 minutes. Allow to cool for 2 minutes, then stir and pot into hot jars. Cover at once. Ready for use in 4–6 weeks.

Pickled Gooseberries

Use firm but ripe fruit for this recipe. Pickled gooseberries make a delicious accompaniment to mackerel and duck.

1.25 kg (2½ lb) gooseberries
750 g (1½ lb) sugar
450 ml (¾ pint) vinegar, preferably white
1 x 5 ml spoon (1 teaspoon) ground allspice
1 x 5 ml spoon (1 teaspoon) ground cinnamon

Top and tail the gooseberries, then rinse and drain them. Put all the other ingredients in a pan, and bring to the boil, stirring until the sugar has dissolved. Add the gooseberries to the pan and cook gently until tender. Remove the fruit from the pan with a perforated spoon and pack carefully into jars. Reduce the liquid in the pan by fast-boiling for 5 minutes, then pour over the gooseberries and cover. Ready for use in 4 weeks.

Pickled Cherries

1 kg (2 lb) red or black cherries
300 ml (½ pint) wine or cider vinegar
1 x 5 ml spoon (1 teaspoon) whole cloves
3 sticks cinnamon
350 g (12 oz) brown sugar

Stalk the cherries, then rinse and drain them. Tie the cloves and cinnamon in a piece of muslin and put in a pan with the vinegar and sugar. Bring to the boil, stirring until the sugar has dissolved. Add the cherries and simmer for 15–20 minutes. Remove with a perforated spoon and pack into warm jars. Reduce the liquid in the pan by fast-boiling for 5 minutes, then pour over the cherries and cover. Ready for use in 4 weeks.

Pickled Crab Apples

Very good with ham, duck or venison.

1. 5 kg (3 lb) crab apples
600 ml (1 pint) sweet spiced vinegar
pared rind of ½ lemon

Choose unblemished fruit of even size, if possible. Remove the stalks, wash thoroughly, particularly round the stalk end, and pat dry. Prick with a stainless steel fork or skewer.

Put the vinegar and lemon rind in a saucepan, bring to the boil and add the apples. Cook gently until almost tender. Watch carefully as, once the skins split, the apples will be too mushy. Remove the apples with a perforated spoon and pack carefully into hot jars. Remove the lemon rind from the vinegar and reduce by fast-boiling for 5 minutes. Pour the vinegar over the apples and cover at once. Ready for use in 4–6 weeks.

Pickled Pears

2 kg (4 lb) pears
600 ml (1 pint) sweet spiced vinegar
500 g (1 lb) sugar
pared rind of ½ lemon

Peel, quarter and core the pears and put in lightly salted water to prevent discoloration. Put the vinegar, sugar and lemon rind in a saucepan and bring to the boil, stirring until the sugar has dissolved. Rinse the pears and add to the pan. Cover and simmer gently until tender. Remove the pears with a perforated spoon and pack into hot jars. Boil the vinegar fast until it has reduced by one-third. Remove the lemon rind and pour the vinegar over the pears. Cover at once. Ready for use in 8 weeks.

Pickled Oranges

Delicious with duck and game.

6 sweet oranges
600 ml (1 pint) water
600 ml (1 pint) sweet spiced vinegar
pared rind of ½ lemon

Scrub the oranges, slice thickly and remove the pips. Place in a saucepan with the water, bring to the boil and cover. Simmer gently until tender.

Transfer the oranges to another pan, using a perforated spoon, and add the vinegar and lemon rind to them. Bring to the boil and simmer gently for 30–40 minutes. Remove the orange slices with a perforated spoon and pack carefully into hot jars. Reduce the vinegar by fast-boiling for 10 minutes, then strain over the oranges. Cover at once. Ready for use in 6 weeks.

Pickled Blackberries

1. 5 kg (3 lb) blackberries
600 ml (1 pint) white vinegar
500 g (1 lb) sugar
25 g (1 oz) ground allspice
25 g (1 oz) ground ginger

Pick over the berries, rinse them gently and drain well. Add the sugar and spices to the vinegar, bring to the boil, stirring until the sugar has dissolved. Add the drained berries and simmer gently for 5–6 minutes. Remove the berries with a perforated spoon and pack into warm jars. Reduce the liquid in pan by fast-boiling for 5 minutes, then pour over the blackberries and cover. Ready for use in 3–4 weeks.

Pickled Figs

500 g (1 lb) dried figs
300 ml (½ pint) malt vinegar
500 g (1 lb) brown sugar
1 x 5 ml spoon (1 teaspoon) ground cloves
1 x 5 ml spoon (1 teaspoon) ground cinnamon
1 x 5 ml spoon (1 teaspoon) ground mace
1 x 5 ml spoon (1 teaspoon) ground allspice

Wash the figs, place in a bowl, cover with cold water and leave to soak overnight. Next day, put the vinegar and sugar in a saucepan, and bring to the boil, stirring until the sugar has dissolved. Boil for 2 minutes, then add the spices and simmer for a further 2 minutes. Drain the figs thoroughly and add to the saucepan. Simmer gently for 45 minutes.

Remove the figs with a perforated spoon and pack into hot jars. Reduce the vinegar by fast-boiling for 2 minutes. Fill the jars so the figs are covered. Cover at once and leave for 4–6 weeks before using.

Pickles for Competitions

If entering a jar of mixed pickle in a show or competition, pack the vegetables in layers according to type. This gives a more attractive appearance to the jar. As with all preserves entered for competitions, no jars of proprietary brand names should be used, the contents of the jar should fill it completely and the jar itself must be immaculately clean and correctly labelled with the contents and date of making.

Drying

FOR CENTURIES, drying and salting were the only known methods of preserving food. Today, in parts of Australia, Africa and California, drying by the sun is still carried out, particularly for fruits such as figs, dates, grapes and also, perhaps to a lesser extent, for apricots, peaches, apples and so on. In certain parts of Europe, fish is dried by the sun and wind.

Fruit and vegetables can be dried at home and little is required in the way of elaborate equipment. Correct and steady temperature and adequate ventilation are the two main requirements.

You will need trays on which to put the fruit or vegetables in a single layer. The trays must be perforated, so that the air, heat and draught can circulate through them. Wire cake trays can be used with cheesecloth or muslin stretched over them and fastened at the corners with pins. Alternatively, you could make a wooden frame with laths; the cheesecloth or muslin can then be stretched across the framework.

Whatever type of tray is used, check that it will fit into the oven. Remember, too, that cheesecloth or muslin has to be thoroughly washed before and after use – even when it is new – so it has to be easily removable from the tray.

Gas, electric or solid-fuel ovens can all be used for drying, provided the oven can be set to a very low heat. Gas is perhaps the least satisfactory, as the heat has to be below that of the lowest regulo setting. If using a gas oven for drying, turn the dial to 0 or ¼ – that is, to the lowest flame possible. It will probably also be necessary to prop open the oven door. In fact, leaving the oven door open can assist in the drying process, as adequate ventilation is necessary to remove the moisture as it is driven out of the fruit. The correct temperature is between 50°C, 120°F and 65°C, 150° F/Gas 0. Where the heat can be regulated and a steady temperature provided, the drying can be carried out as a continuous process, if this is convenient.

With solid-fuel ovens, the heat maintained after cooking sessions can be utilized. This is likely to mean that the drying process is not continuous and has to be carried out over several days but this should not affect the quality of the finished product. It is the simmering oven, in solid fuel cookers, that should be used for drying.

When drying either fruit or vegetables in an oven, check the temperature occasionally during the drying process. As it is very hard to check such low temperatures, even with an oven thermometer (although this is useful to have), a good 'old-fashioned' guide is to put your hand in the oven – you should be able to keep it there in comfort for at least 30 seconds.

Space over hot-water cisterns, in airing cupboards or over a coal range is ideal, temperature-wise, but make sure that there is adequate ventilation and the food is protected from dust. You will probably need to erect a rack or racks in such areas.

Once dried, fruit and vegetables will keep for many months if the drying process has been correctly carried out.

When dried fruit is required for use, allow sufficient time for soaking before cooking (24–48 hours) and use plenty of water. Then heat gently to boiling point in the soaking water and simmer gently until tender. If you want to sweeten it, add sugar a few minutes before cooking is completed.

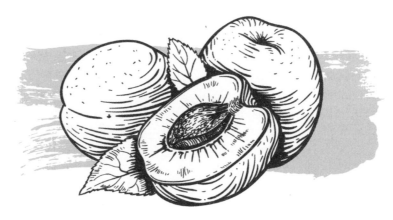

Fruit

As with any method of preservation, it is very important to use good-quality, fresh, ripe fruit. Fruit in the peak of condition will retain a much better colour and flavour. Prepare it according to type (see following instructions), lay it on the trays, and dry at a temperature of about 50°C, 120°F/Gas 0.

Do not allow the temperature to rise above this heat for the first hour, as the outside surface of the fruit will harden, and this will prolong the process of evaporation of moisture from the fruit. It may also cause the skins of plums, apricots and peaches to burst.

When the drying process is completed, remove the trays from the heat and leave to cool at room temperature for 12 hours. Pack the fruit in wooden or cardboard boxes lined with greaseproof paper and store in a very dry place. Do not store in airtight containers.

Apples

Peel, core and slice crossways into rings approx. 6 mm (¼ in) thick. As you cut the rings, place immediately in a bowl of lightly salted water – 1 x 5 ml spoon (1 teaspoon) salt to 1 litre (2 pints) water – to prevent discoloration.

When you have prepared them all, remove the apple rings from the bowl, shake off excess water and pat them dry with a clean tea towel or something similar. Arrange in single layers on trays, or thread on bamboo sticks or dowelling rods cut to fit the oven. Place trays or hang sticks horizontally in the oven.

If the drying process is to be continuous, the apple rings will need 4–6 hours. You can test to see if they are properly dried by pressing a handful of the rings together. They should be springy enough to separate immediately they are released. The finished texture is a little like chamois leather.

Pack the rings in wooden or cardboard boxes lined with greaseproof paper and store in a very dry place.

Apricots

Use large, ripe but firm fruit. Halve and stone them and put the halves in single layers on trays, with the cut surfaces uppermost. Dry slowly at a temperature of 50°C, 120° F/Gas 0. Keep the oven at this temperature until the skins start to shrivel, then raise to 65°C, 150°F/Gas 0.

Apricots take longer to dry than apples, anything between 16–24 hours of continuous drying or longer if the drying is intermittent. Test the fruit by squeezing gently; if no moisture is visible, and the skin remains wrinkled, drying should be complete. Allow the apricots to cool for 12 hours at room temperature before packing as for apples.

Peaches
Halve and stone and dry in the same way as apricots.

Pears
Peel, core and cut into quarters or eighths. Drop into lightly salted water – 1 x 5 ml spoon (1 teaspoon) salt to every 1 litre (2 pints) water. Dry on trays as for apples and pack and store.

Plums
Choose dark-skinned, fleshy varieties. Wash if necessary, drain and leave whole. Place in single layers on trays and dry slowly at an oven temperature of 50°C, 120°F/Gas 0. Keep the oven at this temperature until the skins begin to shrivel (if the heat is too strong at first, the skins will burst and the juice and flavours will be lost). When the skins have started to shrivel, raise the oven temperature gradually to 65°C, 150°F/Gas 0 and maintain this temperature until drying is finished.

Test plums by squeezing one gently between the fingers; if the skin does not break and no moisture exudes from it, the drying process is completed. It will take approximately 20–24 hours. Allow to cool at room temperature for 12 hours, then pack and store as for apricots.

Vegetables

Root vegetables are not worth drying, as they can be easily stored in boxes of peat or sand or in clamps in the garden. But mushrooms, all varieties of string beans, onions and some peas can be dried successfully. Whole onions are usually stored in 'strings' or in nets but a supply of dried onion rings can be useful in late winter or early spring.

Runner or French beans

Choose young, fresh beans. Wash, top and tail and string them. Young beans can be dried whole but older beans should be cut diagonally into strips with a stainless steel knife or coarse bean cutter.

Blanch the beans in boiling water for 2–5 minutes, depending on the age of the beans. If 12 g (½ oz) bicarbonate of soda is added to every 4.5 litres (1 gallon) of the blanching water, it will help to retain the colour of green vegetables but will destroy the Vitamin C content. Drain the beans and spread them out on an old clean tea towel to absorb the surplus moisture.

Spread them out on trays and dry in the oven at a temperature of 50°C, 120°F/Gas 0. Increase the temperature gradually to between 65°C, 150°F and 71°C, 160°F/Gas 0. When dried, the beans should be quite crisp. Depending on their size, this will take between 2–3 hours. Pack them in tightly corked bottles or airtight containers and store in a dark place.

When required for use, soak in cold water for 12 hours, drain, then cook in boiling salted water in the usual way.

Mushrooms

Whether you are using field or cultivated mushrooms, they must be very fresh. Peel them if they are dirty; otherwise just wipe them over with a soft damp cloth. Remove the stalks (use these to make a concentrated stock to freeze for adding to soups and casseroles) and either spread on trays or thread on strings, leaving a small gap between each mushroom. Place the trays in the oven, or hang strings above the boiler or in the airing cupboard. Dry at a temperature not exceeding 50°C, 120°F/Gas 0 until crisp. This will take 6–12 hours. Store in jars in a dry cupboard.

Dried mushrooms can be added, without soaking, to soups, stews, casseroles and sauces. If the mushrooms are required for frying or grilling, soak them first in water or milk for about 1 hour. Pat dry before cooking.

Onions

Choose medium-sized onions. Peel and cut into 6-mm (¼ -in) slices. Separate these into rings but do not try to dry the tight centre circles.

Blanch the rings in boiling water for 30 seconds, drain and dry on an old clean tea towel. Spread in single layers on trays and dry at a temperature of 65°C, l50°F/Gas 0 until crisp and dry.

The drying process, if continuous, will be completed in 3–4 hours. After drying, allow the rings to cool completely. Store in a dry place. When required for use, soak in warm water for about 30 minutes, then use as ordinary onions.

Peas
It is essential that only young peas are used. After podding, the method is the same as for beans. Alternatively, peas may be dried on the vines, as if for seed, then podded and stored in a dry place. However, for this method, the marrowfat varieties are best.

Herbs

Although herbs are best used fresh, it is extremely useful to have a store of dried herbs in the kitchen. Herbs such as parsley, mint, sage and marjoram are often used in large quantities during cooking and a few jars or bunches of dried herbs are an excellent standby to add flavour to soups, stews, vegetables and salads.

Herbs intended for drying should be gathered on a warm, dry day and before the sun has warmed the leaves sufficiently to begin evaporating the essential oils. Pick them just before they come into flower because, after flowering, the leaves start to toughen. Pick and process one variety or type of herb at a time.

Method 1 Pick the herbs and remove any dead or withered leaves. Tie in small bunches by the stems and blanch in boiling water for a few seconds. Shake off any excess water and leave to dry, or pat dry on a tea towel or kitchen paper. Wrap loosely in muslin and hang up to dry in a warm place, such as over a cooker or in an airing cupboard.

The length of time the herbs will take to dry will vary according to the temperature and the draught. If considerable heat is radiating from the cooker, for example, and there is also a good draught, they may be dry in just a few hours. If left in the airing cupboard, where there is little draught, they may take 3–4 days. The drying process is complete when the main stems of the herbs crack, rather than bend, and the leaves are brittle.

Method 2 If using large-leaved herbs, such as mint or sage, strip the leaves from their stalks. Pick over herbs for any dead or withered leaves, then blanch small bunches of leaves (tied in muslin) or sprigs of herbs in boiling water for 1 minute. Shake off the excess moisture, and spread leaves or sprigs on trays. Place in a cool oven, at a temperature between 45°C, 110°F/Gas 0 and 55°C, 130°F/Gas 0. The herbs should be dried until they are crisp; if the drying process is continuous this takes about 1 hour. (On a rack above the stove, it will take 3–4 hours.)

When dry, crush the herbs with a rolling pin, discarding any stalks. If you want to reduce them to a fine powder, sieve them. Store in small airtight containers, well-filled to preserve the fragrance. If stored in glass bottles, protect them from the light to conserve the colour.

Note If drying sprigs or stalks of herbs in the oven, turn them over halfway through the drying period to ensure even drying.

Parsley
This is so useful, it is well worthwhile preserving as much of the colour and flavour as possible. Either of these methods may help:

1. Wash the parsley, if necessary, and pat dry. Hang the stems over the bars of an oven shelf and heat for about 1 minute at 200°C, 400°F/Gas 6. Reduce the heat rapidly and finish drying in a slow oven at 130°C, 250°F/ Gas 0. This takes approximately 15–30 minutes but watch carefully to prevent the parsley scorching.

2. Wash if necessary and pat dry. Tie the parsley in loose bundles and hang in the oven. Dry at a temperature of 115°C, 240°F/Gas 0 for 1 hour. Switch off the oven and leave the parsley in the cooling oven until it is quite crisp.

With both methods, crush the dried parsley with a rolling pin and store in the same way as other herbs.

Salting

SALTING as a means of preserving meat and fish has been used for centuries. Records dating from the Middle Ages tell us of salted beans to go with the salted pork in winter.

Vegetables and nuts are dry salted but the liquid content in vegetables combines with the salt to make brine, so the salt used must be readily soluble. Cooking salt is the best for this purpose. Sea salt can also be used but it is expensive. Table salt is also more expensive than cooking salt and contains chemicals that may form a scum on top of the vegetables.

Allow 500 g (1 lb) cooking salt to every 1.5 kg (3 lb) vegetables and, as with all types of preservation, use good-quality produce.

It is not necessary to fill a jar all at once; it can be filled as the produce becomes available, but always leave it with a layer of salt on top. While the jar or container is being filled, place a weight, such as an upturned saucer, directly on top of the contents.

Equipment

Jars Unglazed earthenware or glass preserving jars (large enough to put your hand in), such as sweet jars, or enamelled containers. It is essential that these are unchipped.
Corks These should be tightly fitting, or use moisture-proof cover, such as plastic tied firmly.
Wooden spoons.

Methods of Salting

Beans
Runner or French may be used, and they should be young, tender and freshly picked. Wash, top and tail, pat dry and remove any strings. French

beans can be left whole; runner beans should be sliced and chopped into 2.5-cm (1-in) lengths.

Always start by putting a layer of salt in the jar, then follow with a layer of beans. Repeat these layers until the jar is full (or you have finished the beans). Press each layer well down as you fill, and always finish with a layer of salt. When the jar is full, cover it with the lid or a saucer for a few days. The beans will shrink and settle, and the jar can then be topped up with more beans and salt. Seal the jar and store in a cool, dry place. (Stone or earthenware jars should not be stored on stone, brick or concrete floors, as moisture will be drawn up into them.)

When you want to use the beans, remove sufficient for your requirements from the jar, wash them thoroughly in several changes of cold water and then soak them for 2 hours in warm water. Do not soak overnight, as the beans tend to toughen if they are soaked too long. Finally, cook in the usual way, but do not add any salt.

Cucumbers

Use fresh, crisp cucumbers. Add 500 g (1 lb) cooking salt to 1.5 kg (3 lb) cucumbers. Wash and dry them, but do not peel. Cut crossways into thin slices – approximately 3 mm (⅛ in) thick – and layer these in a shallow dish, such as a large meat plate. Sprinkle with half the salt. Press down lightly with a plate and leave for 24 hours.

Drain the slices (there will be quite a lot of liquid) and pat as dry as possible with a clean tea towel or cloth. Using a 1-litre (2-lb) preserving jar or similar container, start with a shallow layer of the remaining salt, followed by a layer of cucumber slices. Continue with these layers until all the cucumber slices are used, or the jar is full. Finish with a layer of salt. Seal the jar and store in a cool dry place.

When required for use, remove sufficient slices, rinse in cold running water and leave to soak in cold water for about 1 hour. The cucumbers can be used in salads, as a garnish, or as an hors d'oeuvre.

Hazelnuts

If you have a glut of hazelnuts or the children need something to keep them busy, try this method of preserving. Gather nuts at the end of September or October and spread them out to dry if necessary, either in the sun or an airing cupboard. Throw away any that look as if they may be diseased or have a worm in them. Rub off the outer husk, (you do not remove the shell at this stage), scrub the nuts in cold water and place on trays in a cool oven (50°C, 120°F/Gas 0) to dry thoroughly. Alternatively, leave to dry in a warm, dry place, turning occasionally.

When the nuts are dry, pack them into a wide-necked stone or glass jar, sprinkling with cooking salt as you pack. Give the jar a little shake so that the salt is distributed among the nuts, and finish off with a 12-mm (½-in) layer of salt. Seal the jar and store in a cool dry place.

Salted Hazelnuts

At Christmas time, try oiling and salting hazelnuts to serve as nibbles with drinks, or pack in pretty jars and give as unusual presents. Every 500 g (1 lb) of whole nuts, when shelled, produces about 250 g (8 oz) of salted nuts.

500 g (1 lb) hazelnuts
5 x 15 ml spoons (5 tablespoons) olive oil
2 x 15 ml spoons (2 tablespoons) salt (sea salt if possible)

Shell the nuts and put the kernels in the grill pan. Grill for 2–3 minutes, shaking occasionally. The skins should then rub off easily. Heat the oil in a heavy-based pan. Add the nuts and cook gently until golden, stirring all the time as the nuts absorb the oil. Stir in the salt and continue to cook gently over a low heat until all the nuts are coated with the salt. Turn out on to greaseproof paper and leave to cool. Store in airtight containers.

Salted Almonds

Almonds can be salted in the same way as hazelnuts and are equally delicious. Use unskinned almonds (or buy them in the shell and crack them open yourself). Put the almonds in a basin, cover them with boiling water for 3–4 minutes and then plunge them into cold water for 1 minute. You can then slip off the skins between your thumb and forefinger.

Dry the almonds on kitchen paper and proceed with the salting process in exactly the same way as for salted hazelnuts, using the same ratios of oil and salt.

Crystallizing

THIS method of preservation is perhaps in the luxury class, but fruit treated in this way at home is not only much cheaper than the expensive shop-bought product, it is also juicier and fresher. The process is not a difficult one but it does take time: about 15 minutes a day for 11 or 14 days, depending on whether you use canned or fresh fruit. If you are making candied, crystallized or glacé fruit to give as gifts, allow yourself at least a fortnight for the whole process.

The actual candying process consists of covering the fruit with a hot syrup, then gradually increasing the sugar content of the syrup from day to day, until it becomes really heavy and the fruits are impregnated with sugar. This has to be done gradually, so that the water present in the fruit is slowly extracted and the sugar is allowed to penetrate. If the process is hurried, the fruit will become tough in texture and shrivelled in appearance.

Apricots, pineapple, cherries and pears are among the most successful fruits for candying, as they have a pronounced flavour. Plums and peaches may also be used and home-made candied peel is delicious. Do not candy different varieties of fruit in the same syrup because the individual flavours will be lost.

For beginners, canned fruit is recommended, as the preliminary processing and packing in sugar syrup makes it easier to candy. (The chart on page 199 gives times for both canned and fresh fruit.)

Whether using fresh or canned fruit, make sure it is good-quality fruit, neither under- nor over-ripe, and try to maintain uniformity in the size of the pieces. Halved apricots and plums, quartered or sliced peaches, chunks or quartered rings of pineapple and quartered pears are all suitable.

No special equipment is needed but, if candying several different fruit at the same time, you will need several pudding bowls and two or three saucepans. The bowls should be large enough to keep the fruit completely covered with the syrup. Make sure the fruit is submerged by placing a small plate or saucer on top of it.

Glucose or dextrose can be used in place of part of the sugar. If liquid glucose is used, the weight should be increased by one-fifth.

If a hydrometer is available, it can be used for checking the density or strength of the syrup throughout the process but this is optional. Careful weighing of the sugar and accurate following of the timetable should ensure a successful result.

Equipment

Saucepans.
Scales Metric and imperial.
Bowls Various sizes.
Measuring jug Heatproof.
Cooking tongs and forks.
Hydrometer (optional).
Waxed paper.
Small cardboard or wooden boxes.

Fresh Fruit

After the necessary preparation – peeling, stoning, halving or quartering – place fruit in boiling water to cover and cook very gently until just tender. Tough fruit, such as apricots, may require 10–15 minutes, other more tender fruit will probably take only 4–5 minutes.

Drain the fruit when it is cooked, reserving the liquid. Add the correct amount of sugar specified in the processing chart on page 199 to 300 ml (½ pint) of the liquid to make the candying syrup.

Canned Fruit

Drain the syrup from the can into a jug and make up to 300 ml (½ pint) with water. Pour into a saucepan and add either 250 g (8 oz) sugar or equal quantities of sugar and glucose. Heat gently, stirring until the sugar has dissolved, then bring to the boil.

Put the fruit in a bowl and pour the syrup on top. Make certain the fruit is completely submerged and leave for 24 hours. At the end of this time, pour off the syrup into a pan and add 50 g (2 oz) sugar. Heat gently, stirring until the sugar has dissolved, then bring to the boil. Pour over the fruit and leave for a further 24 hours.

Repeat this process on day three and four (at 24-hour intervals), adding 50 g (2 oz) sugar each time.

On day five, drain the syrup into a pan and add 75 g (3 oz) sugar. Heat gently, stirring until the sugar has dissolved. Add the fruit and simmer gently for 4 minutes. Return the fruit and syrup to the bowl and leave for 48 hours. Repeat this process, at which point the syrup, when cool, should have the consistency of honey. Leave the fruit to soak for 4 days.

Note Fruit can vary in its capacity to absorb sugar, and the density of the syrup in canned fruit can vary, too. If, at this stage, the syrup is still thin and runny, boil it once more with another 75 g (3 oz) sugar, then add the fruit and simmer for 4 minutes.

When the fruit has been soaking for 4 days, drain off the syrup and lay the pieces of fruit on a wire cake tray, placed over a plate to catch the sticky drips. Put the tray of fruit in a very cool oven – not more than 50°C, 120°F/Gas 0 – or in an airing cupboard. Turn it occasionally during the drying period. If the heat is continuous, as in an oven, the fruit will be dry in 24–48 hours, depending on the type and size of fruit; where the heat is intermittent or very gentle, as in an airing cupboard, the fruit may take 48–72 hours to dry. The fruit is dry enough when it is no longer sticky to the touch, and can be easily handled.

Candied fruit and peel will keep for up to 2–3 weeks in the final heavy syrup, so the drying and finishing processes can be spaced to suit the individual.

Any syrups left over after candying fruit are very good as a sauce for ice cream, meringues, or sponge puddings, or added to fruit salads.

You can give the candied fruit a crystallized or glacé finish (or leave it as it is), and then pack it in cardboard or wooden boxes. Use waxed paper to line the box and to separate the layers. Do not seal the containers or make them airtight, as the fruit may go mouldy under these conditions.

Crystallized finish Dip each piece of fruit into boiling water, using cooking tongs or a fork to support the fruit (do not pierce the fruit with the prongs). Shake off excess moisture, then roll each piece in caster or fine granulated sugar. Allow to dry before packing in the same way as candied fruit.

Glacé finish Dissolve 500 g (1 lb) sugar in 150 ml (¼ pint) water and bring to the boil. Keep this syrup hot and covered with a tight-fitting lid to prevent evaporation while fruit is being dipped.

Dip each piece of candied fruit in boiling water for 20 seconds and drain. Pour a small quantity of the syrup into a hot cup and dip pieces of fruit quickly into it, using a skewer or fork. Place the fruit on a wire tray. As soon as the syrup looks cloudy, discard it and use a fresh portion.

When you have dipped all the fruit, place the wire tray in a warm place, where the temperature does not exceed 50°C, 120°F/Gas 0. Turn the fruit occasionally as it dries. Pack in the same way as for crystallized or candied fruit. Fruit given this finish keep juices far longer as the moisture is retained.

Sweetmeats

An old-fashioned but easy sweet can be made from sweetened fruit pulp. Strong-flavoured fruit such as damson and blackcurrant are particularly good, but plums, apples, pears and apricots are also suitable for this method of preservation.

Prepare the chosen fruit, which should be fully ripe, and simmer until soft and tender in just enough water to prevent the fruit burning. Press through a sieve, and return the pulp to the saucepan. Sweeten to taste (some fruit, such as dessert pears, will need little if any sugar). Simmer the sweetened pulp gently until thick, stirring constantly. Spread out in a greased cake tin to a depth of approximately 12 mm (½ in) and leave to dry.

When firm enough to handle, cut into shapes and roll in caster sugar. Pack as for glacé or crystallized fruit.

The addition of a few cloves to apple pulp, or a suitable liqueur to pear pulp, will provide a variation in flavour.

These 'sweets' are good chopped and sprinkled on top of a milk pudding just before serving.

Candied Orange or Lemon Peel

This is a quick method for candying small quantities of peel. Candy orange and lemon peel separately. Homemade candied peel is deliciously moist and makes all the difference to your homemade fruit cakes. Try chopping it with a selection of your crystallized fruit and mixing this with a block of softened vanilla ice cream. Re-freeze the mixture and you will have a 'homemade' tutti-frutti ice cream that beats anything you can buy! Just on their own, strands of candied peel make delicious after-dinner nibbles. Or, for something even more special, melt some plain chocolate in a basin over a pan of hot water and dip the strands of peel into this. Lay them out singly on waxed paper to dry.

Use 50 g (2 oz) sugar to each orange or lemon. Wash the fruit and cut into quarters. Scrape off the pulp (use it for a pudding or fresh fruit drink), then put the peel in a pan and cover with water. Simmer gently for 1–2 hours or until tender. Test a piece of peel between thumb and first finger; it should feel soft and 'squashy' but it should still hold its shape and not break. The water may need topping up during this process.

When tender, add the correct quantity of sugar to the pan, stir until dissolved and bring to the boil. Remove from the heat and allow to cool, uncovered.

Next day, bring the contents of the pan to the boil again and simmer for 4–5 minutes. Remove from the heat and allow to cool, uncovered. On the third day, simmer gently until the peel has absorbed most of the syrup.

Drain the peel and put on a tray to dry. Place in an airing cupboard or at a similar temperature. Any remaining syrup can be poured into the hollow of the peel.

Alternatively, you can give the peel a final coating of fresh sugar syrup, as described in the glacé finish for candied fruit (page 195), before drying. Store in airtight containers in a dry place and use within 6 months.

Grapefruit peel can be candied in the same way but change the water two or three times during the initial cooking process.

Candied Angelica

Candied angelica is invaluable for decorating puddings and cakes and, if you candy it yourself, it will be infinitely more moist and juicy than the shop-bought type. For an unusual but delicious sweet, chop some candied angelica and fold it into a lemon syllabub just before serving. Decorate the top with a few more pieces, and you have a dinner-party pudding par excellence.

angelica stalks
1 x 5 ml spoon (1 teaspoon) salt
1.5 litres (3 pints) water
500 g (1 lb) sugar, or 250 g (8 oz) sugar and 250 g (8 oz) glucose

Pick angelica stalks when they are young and green (in April or May). Cut off root ends and leaves and place the stalks in a basin. Make a brine with the salt and 1 litre (2 pints) of the water. Bring to the boil and pour over the stalks to cover them. Soak for 10 minutes.

Drain the stalks and rinse well under cold running water. Place in a pan of fresh boiling water and boil for 5–7 minutes. Drain, and scrape away the outer skin. Put the stalks in a bowl.

Make a syrup from the sugar, or sugar and glucose, and remaining 500–600ml (1 pint) water. Bring to the boil and pour over the stalks. A little green food colouring may be added to the syrup if desired. Leave for 24 hours.

Follow the chart on page 199 for candying canned fruit until the syrup is the consistency of honey. Dry as for fruit. When finished, roll in caster sugar and store in airtight jars or in boxes lined with waxed paper.

Marrons Glacés

MAKES 1 KG (2 LB)
1 kg (2 lb) sweet chestnuts
water
500 g (1 lb) sugar
500 g (1 lb)glucose
vanilla essence

Choose sound, firm chestnuts and snip the tops to prevent them bursting. Put a few at a time into boiling water and simmer for 2-3 minutes. Peel while hot, making certain that all the brown inner skin is removed. As you peel the chestnuts, put them into a large pan and cover with cold water. When they are all peeled, bring the water to the boil and simmer gently until the chestnuts are tender (test occasionally with a fine skewer).

Put the sugar, glucose and 375 ml (12 fl oz) cold water into a saucepan large enough to hold the chestnuts. Bring to the boil, stirring occasionally, and boil for 1 minute. Add the drained, cooked chestnuts and return the syrup to boiling point. Remove the pan from the heat and leave overnight in a warm kitchen or airing cupboard.

Next day, re-boil the syrup and chestnuts (without a lid). Cover and leave overnight, again in a warm place. Repeat this process, once more, adding 6-10 drops of vanilla essence before heating. Remove the chestnuts with a perforated spoon and drain on a wire rack (placed over a large plate to catch drips). Allow to dry overnight in an airing cupboard.

The chestnuts can be eaten at once but are improved if given a glacé finish, as with candied fruit. If they are to be kept more than 4-6 weeks, they should be wrapped individually in squares of foil.

Crystallized Flowers

This is a very pretty way of preserving flowers and, if properly stored, they will keep for 2–3 months. Choose flowers with clear, bright colours and a flattish shape. Flowers with a bell or trumpet shape are difficult to dry successfully because they lose their shape. Violets, primroses, pansies, carnation and rose petals and apple blossom are all suitable.

There are two methods of crystallizing or preserving flowers but, whichever is used, the finished product should be handled with care.

1.   Flowers must be clean and free of dust. Remove practically all the stalk and, using a small paintbrush, paint the flowers with unbeaten egg white. Paint both back and front of the flowers. Any spots left unpainted will shrivel and may cause mould.

Dredge with caster sugar, back and front, and place on a wire cake tray covered with muslin or greaseproof paper. Dry in an airing cupboard for 24 hours, turning once or twice to prevent the flowers sticking.

2.   Soak 2 x 5 ml spoons (2 teaspoons) gum arabic in 2 x 15 ml spoons (2 tablespoons) rose or orange-flower water in a screw-top container for 3 days. (Gum arabic is available from sugarcraft suppliers.) Shake occasionally and stir before use. Using a small paintbrush, paint the chosen flowers, back and front, as in method 1. Dredge with caster sugar and dry in an airing cupboard for 24 hours, turning occasionally to prevent from sticking.

Crystallized flowers should be stored in boxes or tins between layers of waxed paper and kept in a cool, dry place.

All the flowers mentioned are edible, and make a very pretty decoration for cold puddings or iced cakes.

Timetable for Candied Fruit

Day	Canned fruit	Fresh fruit
1	Dissolve 250 g (8 oz) sugar or equal quantity glucose and sugar in 300 ml (½ pint) syrup from can. Bring to boiling point and pour over fruit. Soak for 24 hours.	Dissolve 175 g (6 oz) sugar or 50 g (2 oz) sugar and 125 g (4 oz) glucose in 300 ml (½ pint) water. Bring to boiling point and pour over fruit. Soak for 24 hours.
2	Dissolve 50 g (2 oz) sugar in syrup, bring syrup to boil and pour over fruit.	As for canned fruit.
3	As day 2.	As for canned fruit.
4	As day 2.	As for canned fruit.
5	Dissolve 75 g (3 oz) sugar in syrup, add fruit, simmer for 3–4 minutes and return to bowl. Soak for 48 hours.	As day 2, canned fruit.
6	Continue soaking.	As day 2, canned fruit.
7	Dissolve 75 g (3 oz) sugar in syrup, add fruit, simmer to make syrup the consistency of honey when cold. Soak for 4 days.	As day 2, canned fruit.
8	Continue soaking.	As day 5, canned fruit.
9	Continue soaking.	As day 6, canned fruit.
10	Continue soaking.	As day 7, canned fruit.
11	Drain and put on wire trays to dry.	As day 8, canned fruit.
12		As day 9, canned fruit.
13		As day 10, canned fruit.
14		Drain and put on wire trays to dry.

Conversion Tables

ALL weights and measures in this book are given in the metric system, followed by the imperial in brackets. Conversions are correctly adjusted within one system and have been taken up or down to round figures in all instances to make for ease of working. Do not worry if you find the conversions differ slightly from those given in the table below, which is for general reference. Providing you follow one set of measures – either the imperial or the metric – these variations are of no importance. Do not attempt to mix the measurements in any recipe, or the amounts will not be correctly adjusted.

Oven Temperatures

These are given in Centigrade, Fahrenheit and Gas Mark.

C	F	Gas	
130	250	½	(very cool)
140	275	1	(very cool)
150	300	2	(cool/slow)
160	325	3	(warm/very moderate)
180	350	4	(moderate)
190	375	5	(moderately hot)
200	400	6	(moderately hot)
210	425	7	(hot)
230	450	8	(very hot)
240	475	9	(very hot)

Weights

Metric	Imperial
25 g	1 oz
50 g	2 oz
75 g	3 oz
100–125 g	4 oz
150 g	5 oz
175 g	6 oz
200g	7 oz
225 g	8 oz
250 g	9 oz
275 g	10 oz
300 g	11 oz
325–350 g	12 oz
375 g	13 oz
400 g	14 oz
425 g	15 oz
450 g	1 lb
900 g	2 lb
1 kg	2 lb 3 oz (approx.)
1·1 kg	2 lb 8 oz
1·4 kg	3 lb
1·6 kg	3 lb 8 oz
1·8 kg	4 lb
2 kg	4 lb 8 oz

Liquid Measures

Metric	Imperial
25 ml	1 fl oz
50 ml	2 fl oz
75 ml	3 fl oz
100–125 ml	4 fl oz
150 ml	¼ pint
175 ml	6 fl oz
200 ml	7 fl oz
225 ml	8 fl oz
250 ml	9 fl oz
275–300 ml	½ pint
575–600 ml	1 pint
1 litre	1¾ pint

Spoon Measures

All spoon measures given in this book indicate level spoonfuls.

Metric	Imperial
5 ml	1 teaspoon
10 ml	1 dessertspoon
15 ml	1 tablespoon

Glossary

acetic acid acid produced by the fermentation of ciders and wines; forms the basis of vinegar.

acid chemical hydrogen compound added to enhance flavour; creates balance with pectin and sugar to cause mixture to jell; aids preservation; used in the forms of lemon juice, vinegar, citric or tartaric acid.

allspice dried berry of Jamaican pepper, used whole or ground as a spice; combines the flavours of cinnamon, clove and nutmeg.

ascorbic acid synthetic form of Vitamin C, used to prevent discoloration of fruit; usually added to sugar syrup for fruit before freezing. Available in powder or tablet form.

bacteria single-celled organisms, capable of rapid growth, which can cause spoilage of foodstuffs.

to blanch to immerse fruit or vegetables in boiling water for a short, specified period of time – to slow enzyme action. The result is to preserve natural colour, flavour and nutritive value.

bottling tongs kitchen tool, useful for removing hot jars or bottles from pan or sterilizer.

brine solution of salt and water, to which sugar, saltpetre, herbs and spices are sometimes added; used to draw water from certain vegetables when pickling. Helps to prevent growth of certain bacteria.

to bruise (fruit) to crush or rupture fruit tissues.

candied peel peel of citrus fruit, impregnated with sugar and dried.

to candy to impregnate suitable fruit with sugar by soaking in hot sugar syrup, which increases in strength over a period.

cayenne very hot powdered spice made from seeds and dried pods of various capsicums (peppers), used to give a hot, peppery flavour.

chilli pungent red or green pod of capsicum (pepper), used fresh or dried to flavour.

chinagraph pencil wax pencil useful for writing on plasticized surfaces, such as freezer packaging.

cinnamon bark of cinnamon tree, used ground or in rolled sticks as a spice.

citric acid anti-oxidant found in lemon juice or available in powder form; prevents discoloration in fruits low in Vitamin C. Also added to fruit deficient in acid to help extract pectin.

clove dried flower buds of tropical evergreen tree, used whole or ground as a spice.

conserve generally, fruits preserved whole in a sugar syrup.

coriander annual plant the seeds of which are used as a spice, whole or round, and the leaves as a herb.

crystallize finish given to fruit after candying, produced by dipping the fruit in boiling water and then into sugar.

to dice to chop into small cubes.

enzyme organic catalyst present in all food which affects the rate at which food deteriorates and eventually spoils. Blanching can stop enzyme action, whereas freezing merely puts the enzymes into a state of suspended animation.

ginger root of a tropical plant, available in root form, ground, preserved and crystallized; used as a flavouring/spice or, if preserved or crystallized, eaten as a sweet.

glacé iced, frozen or glazed. Finish given to fruit after candying, produced by coating the fruit in a very concentrated sugar syrup.

glycerine colourless, sweet, syrupy liquid.

headspace space left at the top of a container to allow room for expansion during freezing or bottling.

to hull to remove stalks and leaves from berry fruit.

hydrometer instrument used to measure the density or strength of liquid, such as sugar syrup for candying fruit.

jelly bag cotton, nylon or flannel bag used to strain fruit pulp to make jelly.

kernel seed, sometimes edible, found inside the stone of stone fruit or inside the hard shell of a nut.

to liquidize to reduce to a purée, in an electric (liquidizer) blender. To make liquid.

mace dried shell of the nutmeg, with a flavour similar to nutmeg, used either ground or in blade form.

macedoine mixture of raw or cooked, diced fruit or vegetables.

micro-organisms generic name for countless bacteria, moulds and other minute organisms, both harmful and beneficial, which are present everywhere.

mould growth on the surface of jam etc, caused by moist air, which can spoil the affected food.

nutmeg seed of a tropical tree, used as a spice. Sold whole or ground.

to open-freeze to freeze fruit and/ or vegetables individually on trays, before packing and storing together. They remain separate and free-flowing rather than freezing together into a solid mass.

paprika mild-flavoured, powdered spice made from sweet red peppers.

paraffin wax substance used for sealing jars containing jam, fruit etc. Obtainable from craft and catering suppliers.

pectin natural substance occurring in fruit and some vegetables which causes their pulp, when boiled with sugar in the presence of sufficient acid, to set as a jelly.

pectin stock juice from fruit such as apples and redcurrants, which are rich in pectin, added to fruit deficient in pectin when making jams or jellies.

to pickle to preserve vegetables and/or fruit in spiced vinegar.

pickling spices commercially prepared mixture of hot and aromatic spices, used to flavour pickles.

pith white substance between the outer rind (zest) and fruit in citrus fruits.

plastic skin substance used for covering jars and bottles. Sold in packets.

to pot to fill jars with jam, jelly etc.

preserving pan large, heavy-based pan recommended for preserving.

preserving sugar type of sugar sometimes used in preserving. The granules are larger than those of granulated sugar and produce brighter and more translucent jams and jellies.

pulp soft and fleshy parts of fruits or vegetables reduced to a moist paste.

purée solid foods made into a smooth consistency by putting through sieve, food mill, liquidizer or masher.

rock salt a salt found in the earth in crystalline form which contains no artificial preservatives. also known as cooking salt.

sea salt a coarse salt, distilled from sea water.

set, or setting point the moment when the sugar and fruit mixture in jams, jellies and marmalades reaches the point of jelling.

shallot perennial plant of the onion family, with a delicate flavour.

to skim to remove scum or skin from the top of a liquid (or cream from the milk).

sorbet flavoured water ice.

to souse to steep or soak in pickle.

to sterilize to destroy harmful micro-organisms from food or cooking utensils, most commonly with boiling water.

sterilizing pan special pan or container, with false bottom, used in some methods of preserving.

stock highly flavoured liquid made from meat, poultry or fish bones, vegetables and herbs simmered in water; used in making soups, sauces etc.

to sugar-freeze to pack fruits in dry sugar for freezing.

sugar thermometer thermometer used in the making of jam, jelly, marmalade, sweets etc.

sweetmeat old-fashioned sweet made from sweetened fruit pulp.

to syrup-freeze to freeze fruits in a sugar syrup.

tartaric acid acid found in many fruit and extracted from wine lees (during the wine-making process). Added to fruit deficient in acid.

turmeric roots of a plant of the ginger family, dried and ground into a bright yellow powder; used as a spice, to colour and flavour food.

yeast microscopic fungus which may grow in certain foodstuffs causing them to spoil. Most readily destroyed by heat and inactivated by cold. Used dried or fresh in baking and brewing.

Index